FROM
SUICIDE
TO SERENITY:

One Survivor's Story

by

Debbie Wilson

ISBN-13 978-1-60145-228-3
ISBN-10 1-60145-228-4

Printed in the United States of America.

Booklocker.com, Inc.
2007

DEDICATION

I dedicate this book to the One who has proven His care and concern over my life, who has comforted me in times of great turmoil, who has given my heart a reason to sing, who has shown me a better way to live, who has straightened my path, and who has given me a connection to the Father I never knew. I love you, Jesus....

Dear Adriene,
my sweet friend,
I have loved getting
to know you. You have been
one of 2012's funnest (+ funniest)
blessings! I hope my book moves
your heart + touches your life in
some small way! Enjoy and take a
4-1/2 hour rest some day soon while
it's still frigid cold out ...haha!
I love you muchly. :)

Love,
Deb Wilson
12-24-12

TABLE OF CONTENTS

PROLOGUE

I am writing this book for survivors of suicide and other tragedies who feel that life will never be better.

I am writing because life does get better.

I am writing for the hopeless or nearly hopeless, because I was that.

I am writing for the lost, brokenhearted, confused souls who feel that the hurts of their heart will not be healed.

I am writing for those who do not know where to begin.

I am writing to the tragedies themselves, in an effort to break their power over us.

I am writing because I can't be still and not write about it any longer.

I am writing because I believe that we human beings help each other along life's pathway, and sometimes in the places least expected.

I am writing because I believe God wants this released to you.

I am writing this out of my personal experience.

For there isn't one thing that could happen to us that God cannot touch, not one tragedy that God cannot heal, not one trauma that God cannot lay His hand upon and make right. There is not one soul, who has deeply loved and lost, that cannot be regained and restored.

This book has been formatted especially with you in mind. You will find quotes at the start of some of the chapters that helped me through that time in my life. The chapters and the book itself are short for a reason. I know what you have been through and I want to relay my story to you in uncomplicated fashion. "Easy on the brain" is the order for the day.

This book is from my heart to yours. My prayer for you is that God will "heal your broken heart and bind up your wounds". May His blessing be with you as you enter into this time of healing.

Love, Deb

CHAPTER ONE:
THE END (AND THE BEGINNING)

"NOOOOOOOOH!", I screamed. "NOOOOH!!!! WHY NOW? WHY COULDN'T YOU HAVE WAITED ONE MORE DAY? WHY? WHYYY?"

My husband had killed himself. He had threatened; I just couldn't believe he would do it. He had scared me before into hiding our gun. Why hadn't I kept it hidden? Why hadn't I stuck to my gut feeling?

Stepping into our living room, I cast a quick glance toward Bob's favorite wing chair. His head cocked to one side, he looked asleep. I thought, 'Oh, that's such an uncomfortable chair to...', then it hit me. I abruptly stopped to try and process what I was seeing.

Oh God, he's gray! No movement. My eyes swiftly moved up to his face again...peaceful resignation. Seconds later, I grasp reality. The other side of his face, mutilated by a .357 magnum. So much blood, his eyeball out of place. I quickly turned away, trying not to look too close; I knew I would be destroyed if I looked too long. A bomb's just been dropped onto my heart. But, most of me wanted to run to him and hold his hand the way we always had, for 15 years.

I had sensed something was wrong as I stepped through the garage door into our kitchen. Our dog, Baxter, whom we had adopted two years before, had always greeted me with a wagging tail. He wasn't in his usual spot, which I thought was weird.

But then, that whole day was weird -- the phone call in the morning at work, the whispered "goodbye", the strange sound of finality in his voice, and my lingering over lunch instead of going directly

1

home, drumming up reasons not to go home. Bob had called me at work wanting to know if I made it all right to work in the fog; I assured him I had. As we continued to chat, I mentioned that I could barely hear him. He was very upset with me when I said that. Previously strong and masculine, his voice had been reduced to a soft-spoken breath.

Little did I know that he was mustering every last ounce of energy that he had to say his goodbye to me, then pull the trigger on his own life.

CHAPTER TWO:
ON SHAKY GROUND

...And you learn to build all your roads on today
because tomorrow's ground is too uncertain for plans.

I carried these words from a poem with me, in my heart and my purse, in the months before Bob died. Unable to rely on the people and things that had always brought me security, life had become an unsettling nightmare. Ten months before the suicide, Bob had taken off on a disability leave of absence from his job as a FedEx courier. Two accidents in his van (and several near misses) convinced me that he was a danger to himself and others on the road. He had started having panic and anxiety attacks as an Operations Manager for the company, then demoted himself to being a courier as the attacks worsened.

I had escaped death, but not major injury, from a severe car accident just a few years before. Three foot surgeries, elbow surgery, and rounds of physical therapy had weakened me mentally, emotionally and physically. I was walking in a lot of pain and felt battered -- by the medical profession, my family, God, and life in general.

Once the diagnosis was made that Bob's disorders were caused by a chemical imbalance and 28 years of alcoholism, I was livid. I was well aware of the drinking problem, but never imagined that our lives would be destroyed by it. Our finances in upheaval, I wasn't even sure we could keep our house. I could hardly deal with my own issues. I was fat, scarred, handicapped, in pain, and overwhelmed with Bob's and my own health problems. And now this: I was a widow, not of natural consequences, but of a suicide. How could he have done this?

My mind reeling, I ran to the bathroom in shock. Still screaming, both on the inside and outwardly, I railed on Bob.

"WHY COULDN'T YOU HAVE WAITED ONE MORE DAY? WHY DIDN'T YOU WAIT FOR THIS DRUG TO WORK? WHY NOW?" But, I already knew the answers.

Bob had been on one mind-altering drug after another for nearly a year, none of which had altered him for the better. His torment had been almost unbearable for me to witness, and I felt increasingly helpless as I watched him deteriorate. The revolving door of psychotropic drugs - Paxil, Prozac, Klonopin, Buspar, Elavil, Triavil, and Lithium – had made him a human guinea pig. Desperate for a functional life, he had tested different dosages of these and other drugs. His condition ranged from drowsy and foggy to enraged and violent. I didn't know what to expect on a daily basis.

The lithium finally calmed his anxiety attacks, but threw him into deeper depression. There was one more type of drug to try, a last-ditch effort when all other drugs fail. It was called an MAO Inhibitor. There were many food limitations with this drug, so we were supposed to go grocery shopping after I returned from work that Monday. I realized, with a sick stomach, that we wouldn't be going anywhere together – ever again.

One by one, Bob's pleasures in life had been coming to an end. Months before, he asked me what my favorite thing in life was, something that I would miss the most if taken away. I told him that I had missed being able to bicycle around a nearby lake after my car accident. I liked being outside, propelling myself with the wind in my hair, and feeding the ducks; I had sorely missed it as I lay in my hospital bed. Bob told me his favorite thing was booze. I stared at him in disbelief. Of all the wonderful things in life to enjoy, not to mention the experiences we had shared as a couple all those years, I couldn't stand hearing that the vodka bottle had been his favorite.

He also loved to eat and, with the new drug, his food would be severely restricted. He told me, "I don't drink any more and now I won't be able to eat either." He felt he was losing his grip on everything, not only the freedom to eat and drink what he wanted, but also his job, his mind, and me.

Bob had entered into an alcohol recovery program five months before he took his life, and the personality changes that followed were profound. He had always been so easygoing and good-natured to live with. Liquor softened him. Once sober (but with the different drugs in his system), he was unpredictable, sullen, out of control. On one drug, he slept endlessly, sometimes 12-14 hours a night, with long naps during the day. When he was awake, cotton-mouthed, dazed, and exhausted, he moved slowly about the house, looking to me for the sanity I couldn't provide. On another drug, he would go ballistic over little things, like my leaving a tuna can on the counter instead of immediately disposing of it. One day while I drove, he made a quick grab for the steering wheel, laying on the horn and screaming at a driver that upset him. My nerves were wracked. Bob had been my 'rock'. I couldn't fathom why God would put me through this, when I couldn't handle what was already on my plate.

In recovery, Bob was forced to face the behavior that he was responsible for -- the hindering of the trust I had for him, damage of our financial security, and troubles in his work and other relationships. This was unfamiliar territory and a difficult process for both of us. He had blamed my car accident and other things for his downfall, and I had allowed it. I entered into recovery with him, attending family nights, and started to learn and embrace my part in the destruction of our lives. I was advised to start emotionally detaching from him, a gut-wrenching and nearly impossible task. We had become almost like one person, unhealthfully linked together.

Moving out of denial, we sought much professional help. We met with a couples counselor, we had AA and Al-Anon sponsors, individual therapists, as well as Bob's recovery program counselor and his psychiatrist to administer the medications.

He felt nothing worked for him, that no one understood his pain. He had been a 'quick fix' type of guy. At that point, there were no fast remedies, only slow struggles with major problems. I was torn between trying to detach, yet knowing how very much he needed me. Our life together was sliding downhill as I watched my once vibrant, quick-witted, bright husband become like a vegetable. I was broken-hearted, frightened, angry, frustrated, and depressed. I wondered what would become of us.

We had always been each other's crutch. When we met, I was 19, living on my own and working two jobs to support myself. My grandmother had been my only real stability, but she had died two years earlier. Bob was 26 and much worldlier than I was. He quickly became my savior and it was a role that fit him. He was overly protective of me, an ex-cop who would shield me from the harshness of the world. I had certainly already experienced it in my young life. I needed to feel safe again with someone who would take good care of me. He readily volunteered, wanting to marry me immediately. He wrapped me in his big arms, the way my Nana had, and my sense of safety returned.

His family life had also been unstable and we clung to each other out of great want and need. We loved and liked each other, and vowed to stick together through all of life's ups and downs. We supported and boosted each other. He grew me up, taking me from a youthful bride of 20 to a woman of nearly 35. After years of consistency and predictability, my savior, my 'rock' had crumbled.

The details of my life would now be in my own hands. Or, so I thought.

CHAPTER THREE:
AFTERMATH

I made the 9-1-1 call, choking out, "I think my husband killed himself." It was dreadful to say that for the first time. The operator told me that I needed to make sure. I thought, 'Please don't make me look again.' With trepidation, I peeked out from behind the kitchen wall, trying to concentrate on the side of his face that had not been blown away. I looked for movement more than anything, but must have caught another glimpse of the blood. I told the operator that I didn't think anyone could survive that. She asked me if there were any reason he would kill himself. I said, "Every reason. Depression, panic attacks, 28 years of alcoholism, no job to go to." She asked what he had done for a living. When I revealed Federal Express, she said, "What is it about that job?" Puzzled, I asked, "You mean with regard to suicide or stress?" It seemed an odd question at an inappropriate time.

I needed to get out of the house, so I took Baxter with me out to the driveway. It was then that the first feelings of relief flooded me. I thought, 'I won't have to deal with this anymore.' Then I felt ashamed to have thought it. My husband lay dead in my home and I was relieved! Later, I would learn that feelings of relief are a very normal reaction to long-term suffering with someone who has placed great burden on you. My next thoughts were of self-preservation: 'Will I have enough money to live on? How will I take care of myself?' Finally, the most profound thought: 'If I don't find God in all this, I never will.'

A nice policeman named Ted was the first to arrive on the scene, then a trained trauma volunteer. Ted put Baxter in the back seat of the police car, and took us to a nearby pizza restaurant where the phone notifications would be made.

There had recently been strained, yet important, communications between my husband and his parents about his childhood. His parents' work life had been hectic, resulting in Bob living in various households. Sometimes he was with his grandparents, other times he would be with people he didn't know. He had felt uprooted and unloved. He was loved, but the circumstances caused much turmoil and were severe for a young boy. Severe enough to begin drinking at the age of 13 to blot out the pain.

Bob and I went through a lot together after my car accident, as well. He hadn't felt supported by his family when I was in the hospital, especially for my third surgery. His father had asked if he should come down (about an hour and a half drive away), but Bob would say he had it all under control. In truth, we were both falling apart and could have used the help, but didn't accept the offer for help. Because of her past, Bob's mother didn't want to intrude on our lives. But, Bob felt that his father should not have to ask, that he should have made the trip out of love as he had for them in their times of trouble.

After so many years of bottling his feelings, he was finally trying to express them to his mom and dad in the months prior to his death. They talked a bit on visits, and worked to straighten out some of his past hurts. He didn't remember a lot about the good times in his childhood. The bad times, and the depression of his life, overrode the good.

I saw much kindness in Bob toward his parents with regard to the decisions they had made for him in his childhood. He knew their lives had also been rough and he didn't want to blame them. Throughout his entire life, he held all his emotional pain inside until he no longer could.

So, when I heard Officer Ted say, "Debbie, Bob's dad wants to know if he should come down", I totally erupted. The reminder of the angst Bob had felt with those words sent me over the edge. I shrieked, "HELL, YES, HE SHOULD COME DOWN! THIS IS HIS SON! HIS SON IS DEAD!," throwing in a few choice words for emphasis. I was out of control, freaking out at that point.

The trauma person was patient, but had little success in calming me down. I called Rocky, Bob's alcohol rehab counselor, and he immediately left his office to join us at the restaurant. He was the most successful in soothing my volatile emotions. We then all went back to the house, where the Coroner had arrived and removed Bob's body. Before we went inside, he gave me Bob's wedding ring and the note that I had quickly skimmed over that had been taped to the kitchen wall.

It read:

August 22, 1994 – Dear Debbie, All I can say is I love you and I'm sorry. I was no longer able to withstand the mental torment that I was going through on a daily basis, I could no longer put on a front that I was holding up ok. The new pills take up to a month to work and the torment has been too bad for too long already. Deb, this will work out better, you can be alone, the insurance money will take the bill worries away. And you can find someone that you're more compatible with. I want you to know that I LOVE you and always have, you can stop feeling manipulated now. Take care of Baxter and the critters, I know you will. Let my folks know that I love them. My life turned out to be such a bunch of shit, I'm so sorry that I dragged you into it. It's like they say, you can't make a silk purse out of a sow's ear. I tried all my life not to be, but I guess I was always a sow's ear. I have some morning agenda, have coffee, write a letter, then take my life, I guess that leaves the rest of the day free. Deb, I don't want to be buried. I want to be cremated and I don't want any services. Please spread my ashes at sea, and pray for me because I don't know whether I'm going to Heaven or Hell. The only friends that need to know are Paul, Roxie, Wally, and Johnson. Deb, it goes without saying that everything I have goes to you. Deb, I LOVE YOU so much I'm going to miss you so bad. Good bye, BOB.

The Coroner wanted to take the note. I told him I would prefer he take a copy, but that wasn't possible. I kept insisting that I get the original back and made him promise repeatedly to return it. I knew I would need it for my healing. I also asked if an autopsy would be performed and he confirmed that it would.

I called a good friend, Annecia, who was like a mother to me. She was massively angry with Bob. She said, "What a legacy he's left you!!" I couldn't bear to hear how mad she was; I protected him by reminding her how much he had suffered.

I had called our other good friends, Jake & Patty, and they drove the hour to our house. It was initially decided that I would stay with them, but they were very concerned for the impact on their children. They told me they would take care of Baxter until everything was sorted out and I appreciated that.

The next decision to be made was where I would stay. I had such difficulty thinking; my brain had already been through so much that day. I knew I would have to stay someplace very quiet, but the friends who first came to mind had noisy households with young children. I didn't think I could withstand the volume. Finally, I thought of Paul & Mary. They were Bob's good and longtime friends from New York. I spoke with Mary on the phone; she was totally empathetic and agreed that I would stay at their home.

We had to lock my cats in one of the bedrooms as the cleaning and restoration company had already been contacted. The only problem was that we couldn't find Casey, my younger cat. Sensitive and skittish as she was, I knew that she must have been traumatized by the sound of the gunshot. There was at least five or six of us in the house looking for her. Finally, Jake pulled her out of the hall closet. She had buried herself under the stair landing in the far corner of the closet.

I was embarrassed that there were so many people roaming around in my dirty house. As Rocky scooped cat litter poops into the toilet, I found myself apologizing for its unkempt state. I told him that I hadn't had much energy to clean lately. He was so understanding and kind; he just did what had to be done and didn't need a job description.

When I arrived at Paul & Mary's house, I cried out all the things to Mary that I had been so desperate to reveal. I had only opened up a little bit to Patty and once to my Al-Anon group. It was such a relief to be able to get my heartache out in the open. I felt like my life had been such a sham, that I had to live it with a happy face on while I was crying on the inside. Mary listened intently. She was wonderfully consoling and took great care of my heart.

Paul finally got home from work, walked in the front door, and shouted good-naturedly, "Okay, who took my parking space?" Mary jumped up from the couch and ran to Paul, telling him the news while I waited in their family room. I heard an anguished "NO WAY!" from him, a voice filled with pain, betrayal, and shock. That triggered my first thought of how much I hated what Bob had done to us.

When bedtime came, no rest came with it. I would sleep 15 minutes at a time, then wake up in disbelief, thinking, "I can't be a widow. He didn't really do this, did he?" He had indeed; I just couldn't accept it. I cried so hard from my deepest hurt.

It was to be the first of many dark nights of the soul.

CHAPTER FOUR:
DETAILS, DETAILS

The week following Bob's death was a whirlwind of activity, which was actually a godsend. The busyness of my days was a good thing. I went about the week planning his memorial service in a daze. There was, mercifully, too much to be done to focus on the heartbreak.

My best friend, Kolene, had driven to me from out of state immediately. Ko and my other friends were of enormous help. I was the final decision-maker on the arrangements, but my friends helped to manage the many details. Jake & Patty made tons of phone calls, Ko & Mary helped to plan the service and ran errands, Gay picked up the food for the luncheon after the service, Ko made sure I had a jacket to wear and worked with me on creating a picture board, assisted with cremation arrangements at the mortuary, and many other small details. I had never planned a funeral or memorial service, so I was wet behind the ears and overwhelmed with the magnitude of what had to be done in just five days.

There were also many family issues I had to deal with. I had been estranged from my mom for fifteen months. Kolene and Mary kept urging me to call her and felt she should know what had happened to Bob so that she could support me. I was in upheaval as to what to do. My brother was wildly alcoholic and out of control, and raged on me over the phone about the suicide. My aunt was dying from her own alcoholism, although I didn't know it at the time. She promised that she would be there for me, at least after the service, to take care of me in my home. I was hoping I could rely on her, but I had serious doubts. My grandma had died 17 years before and I kept thinking, 'If only Nana were alive, she would be here for me.' I needed her more than ever.

I decided to let Kolene contact my mom. She talked to her for several hours a few nights before the service. My mom had a lot of questions about my health, my ankle, and Bob. She kept saying, "That's my daughter. I'll be there." But by the next morning, she had called and left a message for me to call her before she made the trip. She lived in Nevada, about 5 hours away, but was still off work from her week of vacation. I discussed calling her with Jill, my Al-Anon sponsor. She advised praying about it (even though I had no connection with God). I did as she suggested, but I felt like I was praying to the air. Then, I made the call.

The conversation evolved around my mom's hurt feelings. She wanted to know if I hated her, if I wanted her to come to the service. I had very little patience with her neediness, but managed to keep civil. I told her that there was some element of my wanting her to be there or I wouldn't have had Kolene call her. I told her that her showing up wouldn't correct everything that we would have to personally straighten out between us, but that I felt she should be notified, that Bob had been her son-in-law for 14 years, and that I thought she may want to come pay respects to him. She said, "Well, then no, I don't think I'll come down. After all, I haven't seen you and the man in a year and a half and no, I won't come then." My mind raced; it hurt so badly. I said calmly, "Okay, goodbye" in my best 'I don't need you anyway' voice, but I was crushed. I drew a hot bath, lay down in the bathtub, and broke into tears.

I was having issues with Bob's family, as well. Everything Bob's dad said seemed to tweak me upside down. The final straw fell when I found out they would possibly not make it to the service on time (due to picking up a relative from New York at the airport). I went berserk. I screamed at Bob's dad on the phone, "YOU WILL RESPECT HIM IN HIS DEATH AND YOU WILL BE THERE ON TIME!"

Despite the type of death, I wanted the memorial service to reflect Bob's warm personality. I chose our song together, "Babe" by Styx. We had oddly enough danced to this song at our wedding, loving the instrumental part in the beginning. It wasn't until the end of his life, however, that the lyrics became strikingly poignant. They rang of how the time was drawing near, that he must be on his way, how he'd need her love to see him through, and that he would be leaving his heart in her hands. So significant.

There was also a newer song that Bob listened to repeatedly right before his death called "Love, Me" by Collin Raye. Bob asked me what I thought that song meant. It was about two people in love, where one had to move away from the other, both at the beginning and end of their lives. I had no idea how prophetic those words would become, especially the part about not giving up on the other, and how the love would be there until seeing each other again.

Bob had been raised Mormon, but had not remained active in the faith. His parents and grandmother really wanted the service in the Mormon sanctuary. Internally, I fought a lot with having a service at all, since it was his express desire in his last letter to not have one. But bottom line, we didn't get the luxury of a goodbye and we all needed it badly. I knew it was important to them to have it in the Mormon church. I was told that the purpose of the memorial service is to bring closure and comfort to the living. That made sense to me, so we moved ahead with the service in the Mormon sanctuary.

My friend, Patty, had called Bob's Mormon ward in New York right after his death and asked if they could be of any help to me. They said they could. A local ward sent over a sweetheart of a woman named Connie, who helped me tremendously with advice on all the arrangements.

I didn't do so well with the bishop. He found it inappropriate to play the music I had chosen for the service in the sanctuary. We listened to the songs together on a trial run, but he thought the middle of 'Babe' was too much rock & roll, and not sacred. I explained the history behind the music and why I felt it was so important. He then took me on a tour all over the church facility in an effort to get to me to agree to another room for the service. He showed me the basketball gym and the tiny Relief Society room as alternatives. The first thing I saw in the gym were the filthy walls from where the balls hit. The Relief Society room was very small and would only accommodate a maximum of 25-30 people. We would be having 80-100 attendees. I was really upset and told him that no one would care about the music. I told him that relatives would be coming in from New York, Bob's grandma and other relatives from San Diego, and that no one would really care about the music, that they would just be grateful to get the goodbye. I thought it was disrespectful to consider having it anywhere else but the sanctuary. I wished Ko & Mary were not in another city picking up Bob's urn and ashes. By this time, I had had five nearly sleepless nights and I was too tired to be going head to head with a bishop the night before Bob's service.

I had already been dragged through the mill, and I felt like I was dealing with a person who seemed to be getting perverse enjoyment out of disrupting my soul, not that my sensitivity wasn't a major factor during that time. We finally ended up praying about it, and he agreed to allow the music on low volume if he could throw in a couple of hymns. I agreed, even though Bob wasn't a "hymn" kind of guy. I needed the service to be as personal to Bob's true self as it could be, but I was willing to compromise, mainly out of exhaustion.

Even though I didn't know how to pray or know God, Jill told me to ask for guidance on where to release Bob's ashes. I had thought of Cambria, but that was more my favorite place than his. One night that week, I released the question to Whoever was listening and, the next morning, I had my answer. I woke up, knowing that it had to be Mendocino, above San Francisco, where we had spent time on vacation, renewing our wedding vows on our 10th anniversary just four years before. Bob's time of greatest peace had been there and I knew that was where I needed to go. It was interesting that I was already getting a sense that there was a God watching over my trying situation. He was providing my answers and moving me as smoothly as possible through everything I was going through.

I told friends that I felt God had spared me, maneuvering Bob's face so that I would not have to meet with full facial horror when I found him dead. I felt there was grace extended to me in the way his face had fallen, the seconds I thought he was actually sleeping, viewing the undamaged part of his face, the gray skin, then the damaged side. I felt that God gave me extra moments to adjust psychologically before the trauma and shock set in. I felt that He had protected me.

His protection was also evident in the incredible amount of support around me through my network of friends and acquaintances. God gave me people who really cared about me, who had suffered from depression and could explain what Bob had been going through, others who had been through alcoholism and suicide attempts, those who worked with addictions, and people whose loved ones had died – both from natural causes and suicide. There was an amazing array of souls around me who could help me sort through the suicide.

It was becoming evident to me that there was a God who knew exactly what I needed and would help me every step of the way.

CHAPTER FIVE:
UNCAUGHT CLUES

The tide recedes but leaves behind
Bright seashells on the sand,
The sun goes down, but gentle warmth
Still lingers on the land,
The music stops, and yet it echoes on
In sweet refrains...
For every joy that passes,
Something beautiful remains.

Bob gave me this poem shortly before he died. I was in our home office, preoccupied with the manuscript I was typing for an author, in an effort to bring in more money. He interrupted my work, gave me the paper, then stood at the doorway while I quickly read it. I looked up and said, "It's beautiful, but what does it mean?" He stared at me and said nothing. I said, "Where did you get this? I know you didn't write it". Bob didn't like to write and was not naturally good at it. He snapped at me that he could have written it. I told him that it didn't sound like him, his style. He lingered for a moment at the door with a strange expression on his face, then he walked away.

It was a weird moment, but I had gone through so much weirdness with him already that I chalked it up as another 'one of those things'. I didn't know it was a clue I was supposed to get. There was no way for me to "get" it. Suicide had not been part of my vocabulary or my experience in life. However, when I re-read the poem after his death and realized the finality of the words in the last two lines, I became wracked with guilt that I had not "figured it out" at the time and done something with the information.

As I thought back to the week prior to his death, it became apparent that there had been more than one of those moments. Just two nights before the fatal Monday, I thought I heard someone trying to get into our home in the middle of the night. I awoke Bob and he immediately went for the gun, but it was not in its usual place. He always kept it in the nightstand beside our bed. On that night, he started looking in the nightstand then went straight for the armoire, searching beneath piles of clothes in his pajama drawer. It was odd that the gun was in a different place. The next day, I had a feeling that I should hide the gun again. I had hidden it before, throwing it up into a box in the rafters in our garage. But this time, I didn't.

Our last Sunday together was one of the best days we had in a long time. We laughed through "Cool Runnings", a movie about the Jamaican bobsled team. It felt good and right to laugh with him for a change; I didn't know it would be the last one we would share.

CHAPTER SIX:
THE SERVICE

*"When people are loving, brave, truthful,
charitable, God is present."*

Harold Kushner

The memorial service was meaningful and beautiful. My friend, Lisa, remarked that it was special, and that I had made it personal and a tribute to Bob's life in spite of all my pain. I appreciated hearing that; any boost to my self-esteem was so needed. Another friend gave me a little note card with the above quote in it. She told me that she very much felt the presence of God, and that these qualities were exhibited in spite of the circumstances.

I had asked Bob's two best Federal Express manager friends to give his eulogy and the sharing. I asked them to keep it light, that I didn't want the service to be morbid. I was so grateful that they revealed funny things Bob had done. Bob was an extremely funny man and I enjoyed hearing how others enjoyed and loved that quality in him. Jake, who gave the eulogy, had his wife, Patty, pull open the Bible on their drive to the service. There were several scriptures that they found, which he shared. The first was, "Clothe yourselves with compassion, kindness, humility, gentleness and patience." The second was, "Dear children, let us not love with words or tongue, but with actions and in truth." He said that these passages fit Bob well. I cried when I heard them, and I agreed. One of the things I loved most about Bob was his kindness and willingness to help. He was a caring man.

The two songs I chose were hard to hear. The volume had been set too low and there was a problem with the sound system. Even that apparent glitch turned out to be perfect. One of my friends told me that she had to listen very closely to hear the words, which made the lyrics more meaningful.

My own sense of humor burst out in huge, inappropriate ways as the attendees came up to me. I found myself saying to his AA friends, "Don't let this happen to you, too!" These were awkward moments, for them and me, yet I was dealing the only way I knew how...through a wacky sense of humor.

Everyone was saying how good I looked, and that I was holding up well. I couldn't believe it. My heart felt shattered into 3,000 pieces, I was in pain walking because of my injured ankle, and I felt heavy by my excess weight and the emotional burdens my heart was carrying. I also didn't know how I would get through life without my anchor. Appearances are one thing, then there's what is really going on inside a person.

There were about 80 people at the service, some that I hadn't worked with in 12 years who came to support me. That was amazing to me, and I felt loved by their presence and comments to me. I was so grateful for all the friends present, because none of my own family showed. I kept thinking that there should be at least one family member there for me, that it would have seemed more right if even one had shown up. I sensed my friends would have to become like family during the road of recovery that lie ahead.

I wished Bob could have seen how many people truly cared.

CHAPTER SEVEN:
PICKING UP THE PIECES

I was invited to share my story at Rocky Hill's family night. I had been attending weekly with Bob and had come to know the other alcoholic people and their families. Amidst the identification process that night - "I am John and I'm an alcoholic; I'm Scott and I'm an alcoholic", I found myself saying, "I'm Debbie and I'm not sure what I am anymore." As I shared my intense grief, I looked around the circle of pained faces as they discovered what I had really been through.

Bob and I had been so good at putting on the "happy face" masks. Now, I no longer had to hide the truth from people. I could be 100% honest, for the first time in my life, and the words spilled out from me. I talked about starting to pick up the pieces of the 'wreckage' he left. That seemed an appropriate word for it...my life felt like a train wreck. I talked about having nearly no sex life in our 15 years together and wanting someone that way. I talked about Bob wearing Depends diapers at night, drinking so much that he couldn't wake himself to use the bathroom, wetting the bed instead. It was cathartic to finally open up those painful years.

I had been told that most suicide survivors don't verbalize their emotional pain, due to the shame factor and societal stigma. I decided against that immediately. I sensed that I would perish from the pain inside me if I didn't keep getting it out of my system. I carried profound guilt for not being able to save Bob, but there was another part of me that knew I had done everything I could to help him, everything that I knew <u>how</u> to do at the time.

I stayed at Paul and Mary's house for the first week and a half, and then they were having company. My house was being restored, the carpet pulled up, the walls repainted, and the furniture removed. It wouldn't be livable for some time, yet Kolene and I were not to leave for five days to fly up north to Mendocino to spread Bob's ashes. Tom, Bob's counselor, invited me to stay at their home, but I didn't feel comfortable with the idea, not knowing him or his family very well. I thought of my other friends, but they had such noisy households. I ended up calling the local DoubleTree Hotel and asked if I could bring my cats to stay with me there. They agreed after I explained the circumstances.

I managed to complete insurance paperwork, make phone calls, and do all the things needed to "take care of business" during that five days. But it was a frightening time, and I felt alone and scared in the hotel room. In hindsight, I see that I should never have been alone during that time. One night, I walked past the bathroom mirror and saw my face half blown off like Bob's had been. I freaked out and immediately called my Al-Anon sponsor, who talked me down from my hysteria. Hanging up, I wondered how much I would have to go through and if I would make a full recovery.

The time finally came to fly to Mendocino to spread Bob's ashes. I met Kolene at the airport. Connie from the Mormon Church had advised us to try to have fun with the trip. So, we decided to make our way first through the Napa Valley wine country since Ko had never seen it.

I had a serious problem with Kolene's chatter. My brain felt so blown apart that I couldn't deal with a lot of talking, unless it was my own venting. Very quiet people who honored my emotions and listened to my pain helped me the most during this awful time. But, I so appreciated Kolene's support as I was not looking forward to this morbid task or making the trip alone.

I had contacted the minister, Lee, who had officiated at our vow renewal. I told her I felt that I needed to stay in a room where I could hear the ocean. I would later learn that the sound of waves is healing. That explained why I felt compelled to drive to the ocean repeatedly as I went through the worst of times with Bob. Apparently, the sound of the waves had a soothing effect on my frazzled nerves.

There were many places with an ocean view in Mendocino, but Lee could not think of one that was close enough to hear the waves. Telling me she would do her best, she called a few days later and revealed that Little River Inn had come to mind. Apparently, there were only two rooms in the area where the waves could be seen and heard. She remembered that she had met an engaged couple in one of those rooms during a pre-wedding discussion.

It was so difficult to be there. Bob and I had eaten dinner at the inn on our anniversary night four years before. Ko and I sat in the same lovely restaurant for dinner, being serenaded by a guitarist, as memories of my time there with Bob flooded me. Kolene loved the ambience; I was just miserable.

My room was big and lonely. Pressed by the need for quiet, I didn't want to share it with Kolene, so I arranged for her to be in a separate room. I had a very restless night, tossing and turning, waking up many times, going to the bathroom, staring at the urn on the floor. I was haunted by it, tormented by what I would have to do the next day.

Lee told me to call her when I was ready for her and her husband, Dick, to take me to a private cove to release the ashes. It was 11:00 the next morning and I wasn't even out of bed yet. She called me and, once she heard my voice, knew I wasn't doing well. She advised me to go down to the restaurant and order a potato, cheese and vegetable concoction that the chef would make especially for me, carbohydrates being the "order for the day". I finally managed to drag myself to the restaurant, then Lee & Dick picked me up and drove me to the cove.

I will never forget Lee's gentleness and respect for me. She asked if I would like them to join me, but I declined. She told me that they would stay over to the side by the ocean on a bench, yet some distance from me, to be a part of the event, yet maintain the separateness. They would be close enough to call if I needed them. I loved the way she handled that.

I walked some distance out in the sand, sat down on a boulder next to the ocean, and talked to Bob for about 45 minutes. I shared my turmoil with him, and told him what he had put me through already. I told him I hated him and loved him at the same time. When I was finished talking to Bob, I asked God for a sign that Bob was in the right place. Everybody and their grandmother had already started coming forth with opinions on whether he was in heaven or hell, and the mental torment was too much for me. I didn't even know if I would be able to detect a sign, but after I asked for it, two sea lions popped their head out of the water. I instantly remembered that Bob and I had seen two sea lions popping their heads up in the ocean behind us during the videotape closing shot after our 10th anniversary vow renewal! Their surfacing at that very moment pierced my heart so powerfully that I burst into tears. I was amazed that God had given me such an obvious sign and I thanked Him for supplying it.

I then released the ashes into the water, expecting they would look like barbecue ashes. I was a little shocked that they resembled cat litter. My offbeat sense of humor wove its way into the event. I thought, 'Bob never did like to scoop the cat box, so here I am handling it again....'. It seemed funny at the time and lightened up my heart a bit. As I chuckled, I felt grateful to still have a sense of humor.

I didn't know God's heart at all then, but I believed the sea lion event was not a coincidence. I had been given much-needed peace of mind at a crucial time.

Lee walked me back to their car and shared with me about her first marriage to an alcoholic man. She likened it to being in a field full of land mines, never knowing where to step to avoid the certain explosion. I understood the analogy perfectly, appreciated the connection with her, and felt comforted by her presence.

Rejoining Kolene at the inn, we decided to look through some of the quaint Mendocino shops before leaving the next day. Preoccupied with what I would face when I returned home, I glanced up and saw a little plaque in a store that said, 'Those who love are never alone'. I stared at those words over and over, then decided to buy it. Somehow, I knew I would feel very alone on the road that lie ahead.

CHAPTER EIGHT:
STAGE ONE - UNDONE

I had no job, no family, no children, nothing to live for now except to take care of my animals and try to discover how to heal my pain, find God, regain myself, and obtain the answers to all the "W" questions that were coursing through my head. Why had Bob done this to me? Why did God kill him? Would those close to me be able to help me through my horrible loneliness? Would they be enough to get me through this? Why did God hate me so much? Why did God put me through the worst stuff – an unstable, alcoholism-filled childhood, the debilitating car accident, the suicide?

Recovery would be a tall order; I didn't even know where to begin. I had instantly contacted the therapist I had seen after my car accident, Cynthia. She helped me through the initial trauma and promised that she would not let me fall. She told me she would call me and make herself available by pager for my calls, even after hours.

My emotions were fluctuating wildly – I was guilt-ridden, anxious, depressed, relieved, enraged – sometimes all within the same 10 minutes. I made the mistake of asking everyone for his or her opinion of what to do to help myself, and this added more confusion to my inner chaos. Cynthia told me to limit the number of my confidantes to five – to carefully select and only discuss my personal issues with those people.

I was so scared of what was going to happen to me, how much my brain was tweaking, and what I may do to myself. It was suggested that I be hospitalized at this time, by a clergy member whom I trusted but who was brand new to my life and didn't know me very well. She recommended one of those nice places where you get medicated a lot and get plenty of sleep.

There was no doubt that my brain was on overdrive; I felt completely insane. I even went to several sessions of a suicide recovery group during this time, but I was raging and they didn't know what to do with me either. Cynthia felt that the "beds & meds" type of hospital wasn't right for me, and that to shut myself up during this time wasn't the proper diagnosis.

My friend, Tawny, had spent the first night with me in my home after the trip to Mendocino. A short time later, Pat, a supervisor I had worked with years before, who was a long-time recovering alcoholic and previously suicidal person, also spent the night. Because of her similar story, she shed new perspective, listened to my hurts, and helped me enormously. It was so beneficial to have someone in the house.

Tawny encouraged me to host two Japanese girls through a foreign exchange program just 5 weeks after Bob's death. It seemed like it was too soon and an overwhelming task for me. I knew I wasn't stable, I was trying to work part-time at a job I had just started 3 weeks prior to the suicide, I was terribly exhausted and depressed, and my home wasn't put back together yet. However, I did have a wonderful loft room that was not being used and the idea was intriguing. I had wanted to host a student years before when Bob was alive, but we never had. This would be a new experience, a way to fulfill something I had always wanted to do, and a way for me to distract from my own pain a little. It was to be a short-term stay, only ten days, so I finally agreed. That would prove to be a wonderful decision.

The girls' needs took some emphasis off of my grief, at least during the day. Rie was lively and spirited, and I loved her energy; Noriko was considerably quieter. Each night after dinner, I would retire to my bedroom, slink down on the floor beside my bed, and break into tears. One night, Noriko decided to try out the swing on my back porch, just outside my bedroom sliding glass door. She glanced over, our eyes locked and it was a most awkward moment, but my grief had made me more of a 'real' person. My sorrow was acutely inside me, and I didn't want to pretend that it wasn't.

I treated the girls to shopping excursions, church, a small plane flight over our community, dog walks in the park, and barbecues at various friends' houses where they would teach us all origami. Our time together was full and lovely. They were two wonderful 20-year-old girls, dental hygiene students, with the sweetness of much younger children.

Noriko ended our visit by writing me the most incredible letter of how I had impacted her life and read it to the group at the bus stop right before they left. I cried hard, then asked their interpreter to tell them how Bob had died and how much their visit meant to me at that time in my life. They broke down when they heard it.

Their visit in my home had been the most positive experience to happen in a flurry of negatives and I could see how life didn't have to be completely miserable. I was beginning to truly understand the words on the plaque I had bought in Mendocino. Although the girls and I had a great language barrier, our communications were based in love. It warmed my heart to know that I had not lost the love inside me through Bob's actions. He had not destroyed the best of me. By placing the love inside me into others, I was starting to see that I could heal and go on.

My foot doctor's nurse, Kandi, got me excited about decorating country style and I started looking for couches. Months later, I was still indecisive about keeping my home and what to do with it. My whole life seemed on hold. I would make plans to do something, then be exhausted and not able to fulfill obligations from the weariness of my grief and depression. My sleep pattern was erratic. There were many nights that I cried for hours, then drifted off to sleep. Some nights, I couldn't sleep a wink. I didn't want to become addicted to a sleep medication, but I asked my foot doctor for something mild and non-addictive. I was prescribed Ambien. I was overly anxiety-ridden, but the drug, combined with soothing creek music, usually helped me to get a good night's sleep.

Nurse Kandi was Christian, and she and her husband tried to lead me into a relationship with Jesus during this time, but I was too hostile with the idea. I still felt that their God had taken the most important thing in my life away from me. I had a small measure of faith that my life would turn out all right, but that sense was often fogged over by the intense emotions and grief I was dealing with. I was going through hell. Oddly enough, on the roughest of nights, I would sleep with the Bible on my bed and chest. There was something inside me that knew this book was the truth about God.

The Bible was particularly beneficial during one bad time. The receptionist at my new job had befriended me, I had opened my heart and guts to her in my trauma, then she started stealing large bills from my purse. I would go to lunch and notice that I still had the smaller bills in my purse, but the $10's and $20's were missing. I was being sent out on short errands and leaving my purse at the office during this time. I had trusted her and was hurt and betrayed by this. I had only been there a short time when Bob shot himself, and I was talking crazy and feeling muddled when I returned. But, those thefts triggered serious paranoia in me. I obsessed that she had gotten hold of my social security card or bank account numbers. At the same time, I couldn't find my extra house key; I thought she had stolen it. I lay awake that entire night, aware of every noise surrounding my house. I opened the Bible on my bed to a scripture that stated all men are liars. I could relate to that.

I turned the pages and my eyes came to rest on this verse:

"The cords of death entangled me,
the torrents of destruction overwhelmed me,
the cords of the grave coiled around me;
the snares of death confronted me.
In my distress I called to the Lord;
I cried to my God for help.
From his temple he heard my voice;
my cry came before him, into his ears."

I cried to Him for help right then. Then I read on:

"He reached down from on high and took hold of me;
he drew me out of deep waters.
He rescued me from my powerful enemy,
from my foes, who were too strong for me.
They confronted me in the day of my disaster,
but the Lord was my support.
He brought me out into a spacious place;
He rescued me because he delighted in me."

Could this be true? Could God rescue me from this hell in my mind? I wanted so badly to believe it. This was truly the voice of God. But there was another voice in my head that said I wasn't going to make it through all this. I was so afraid that my mind was short-circuiting and that I would hurt myself, not even knowing what I was doing. I promptly went out to my kitchen and put the large kitchen cutting knives in the garage, so they would be farther away from me. There was nothing else that resembled a weapon in the house to hurt myself with. I felt at peace after that.

Very early the next morning, I called a locksmith and had him rekey my home and add some extra security items. I flew into my bank right as they opened and explained that my accounts would have to be changed, with myself as the sole signer. I told them what happened at work and that I knew it all sounded like a Movie of the Week, but my fears were real to me and my life insurance settlement was the only thing I had to help me get through the suicide. They were understanding and empathetic, and a teller named Stephanie gave me her business card in case I should need to talk.

My brain broken apart, I ended up on Rocky Hill's doorstep next. I revealed to Rocky's wife, Deb, what had happened, along with other paranoid concerns I had. She spent an hour and a half with me, talking me down, and tried to assuage my extreme fears. I was so thankful for her and felt that God was watching over me, bringing me the human angels I needed to help me through this haunting time.

Not being able to process my thoughts properly, I had made weird comments at work and it was becoming clear that I wasn't equipped to be in a workplace. The other employees started giving me the silent treatment in an effort to get me to quit. I knew I had to (and I did), but it was still hard because these people had promised to be a second family to me after they heard of Bob's death. The theft of the money and their ill treatment was too much for me. It led to an uncontrollable freaking out in my home shortly after, pacing the floor, knowing I needed someone to talk to, but not knowing whom to call.

It was at that very moment that my dog groomer and new friend, Louise, rang my doorbell. She handed me a small piece of paper. I looked down at it and read, "There's a Reason for Everything," a poem that explained God's purposes in suffering. I broke down in crying jags, then told her what happened at work, as well as other confessions laying heavily on my chest. It felt so good to vent to her. She allowed me to get everything bothering me out in the open and listened to me earnestly. Then, she told me, "It doesn't really matter what these people think of you. They don't even know you. It's nothing; they don't mean anything." I carefully thought that over, and knew there was truth in what she was saying.

Her care for me in taking the time to listen and her hugs on me wound my emotions down. Another angel, thank God.

CHAPTER NINE:
THE CHURCH SEARCH

"Nurture strength of spirit to shield you in sudden misfortune."
- Desiderata

Shortly after the suicide, my Al-Anon sponsor, Jill, told me about a "different" kind of church, one that she occasionally attended. I was desperate to find God, so I went with her the next Sunday. The service was sweet and non-threatening. Even the style of the building's architecture was appealing and exactly how I envisioned a church should look. It was a very old building, with a powder blue door and stained glass windows that housed the words 'Love', 'Integrity', 'Peace' and other nice words on them, combined with beautiful scenes. The female minister was wonderfully warm and loving. I felt good there, at home. Bob's alcohol counselor also attended with his wife and children. I was clear that I did not want religion or Jesus to be shoved down my throat at this point. A "holy roller" church was out of the question. I didn't feel that my shattered brain would be able to handle it.

Workshops were conducted there from time to time. They seemed more psychological than spiritual. Cynthia felt this type of church was of value to me. The people were very loving to me. The problem was in the spiritual counseling. Guest speakers visited, gave the message and made themselves available for counseling, along with my minister. What they advised was frustrating and impossible to accomplish. They would tell me to calm down and meditate at a point in my life when my emotions were raging and out of control, I had no connection with God, and all of life's unanswered questions were still wreaking havoc on my brain.

The church members would tell me that God really loved me. I wondered why they believed that, what proof they had. They were never able to clearly point to anything that would make me believe it with any certainty. I certainly didn't feel it and, as month after month went by, my darkness deepened as I tried to understand through this church and New Age books why my life had taken the turn it had.

The New Age movement believes that everything is good. It didn't make sense to me that an event with such traumatic effects as the suicide was a good thing. I struggled to understand and find answers that I could believe in that actually fit. But there seemed to be hundreds of puzzle pieces scattered all over the floor of my life. I would read books that talked about consciousness, metaphysics, Spirit….but the words gave me nothing SOLID to lean on, learn from, sink into. Bob had been God to me, and now that he was gone, I was desperately searching for the real thing. The New Age teachings confused me more, and I kept fighting to find energy to diligently read, learn, and to find answers when my brain just needed a rest.

Even when I allowed myself this rest, I didn't stop for long because the search for God was too important. I felt that my very life depended on it. I was afraid what would happen to me if I stopped, so I kept moving although exhaustion was taking over my body. I attended a few other more traditional churches during this time, but nothing clicked for me. My friend, Michele, told me that I sighed a lot during this time, as if I was bearing the weight of the whole world on my shoulders. That's what it felt like. My guilt, rage, confusion, and depression were weighing heavily on me. The constant sighing pulled oxygen into my body so that I could go on.

Especially during the first six months of recovery, people from various churches would knock on my door. I felt bombarded from every direction and turned off, like every church in town was after me. Jehovah Witnesses that I had come to know witnessed to me in my home before Bob died. They taught me why the Bible had God's answers, calling it the perfect guidebook for life. I did not know at the time that the Bible they use is rewritten, altered to support the beliefs of their organization. They were friendly and supportive people, but I needed firm answers about God, His love, and why bad things happen to good people. Although they provided answers that made some sense to me, I was not convinced they had the complete truth. They seemed more about religion and work to me, and I was looking for a personal way to God in which I could completely KNOW that I was connected.

There were some elements of truth in their teaching, however, and I took what they said into my New Thought church's Bible class. One night, I mentioned how the artifacts from archaeological digs supported what was in the Bible. The minister was tight-lipped and not receptive to what I had to say. At the end of one of our classes, she read from The Lord's Prayer the line, "Lead us not into temptation, but deliver us from evil". She was totally stumped about this line, and was unable to break it down and explain it. Because this church and the New Age movement believe there is no evil, there was no explanation. When she revealed that spirituality wasn't about "some bloody dead guy on a cross" but that His teachings were valuable, the hardness in her heart and voice didn't escape me. I didn't understand completely, but I knew people who had a real connection with God, and Jesus seemed to be the key.

However, I was determined to save my own life; I did not want a Savior. Nevertheless, there was something different, SOLID, about the people who shared their lives with me, telling me about Jesus' love for me. I observed the authority with which they spoke and I noted a softness in their souls toward their Lord. There was a steadiness in their lives and beliefs, and a truth that shone through them that was undeniable. It was almost impossible to believe that Jesus loved me, with everything I had gone through, but there was a part of me that wanted so badly to believe it. Instead, I hardened my heart to these sweet messages and continued my search, trying to find more "suitable" answers for my life. After all, I was open-minded, a broad thinker. I wanted to be developing my spirituality on a path which was tolerant of ALL people, not just Christian religious people, and I believed that this path was way too narrow for my broad mind. I didn't want a rigid religion to control me.

I determined there must be a better way to God, but I also knew the truth was most important. I started praying for God not to let go of me until I had the "truth" of Him. My heart stayed on course and I literally consumed dozens of books about suicide, grief, and people's opinions about God. I was on a mission to learn the meaning of life, the truth about God, the way to God, and His purpose for me through my tragedies.

I started college five months after Bob died, in an effort to find myself and what I wanted to be when I grew up. It was so difficult to focus, but I achieved straight A's. My studies, however, interfered with what I felt was my most important task in life– finding God.

CHAPTER TEN:
A SAFE HAVEN

It wasn't long before acute loneliness became my constant companion. I thought I would just go crazy if I had to spend another moment alone. I felt too insane to work, and I was. My friends were available by phone and an occasional outing or meal, but I could see that I was not doing well on my own. I just wanted Nana, my precious grandma, to be in my home to comfort and stay with me. There certainly was a connection between her and Bob. Although they had never met, her love reminded me of his. They were identical in the way they both cooked for me as a show of their love, the way they rubbed my back, and the way they took care of me. I sensed that I needed someone to stay with me, and believed that if I had just had one family member willing to do so, things would have felt more stable. But, Nana had been dead for seventeen years, Bob was now gone, and I felt like an orphan, all alone in the world.

As God would have it, there was someone out in the world who was deeply hurting for me. This was Michele. She had been my home health physical therapist turned friend after my car accident three years before, but I hadn't maintained our friendship. When she learned of Bob's death, she wrote me a card and letter about Bob, what he had meant to her, and how his kindness, through the midst of his own pain, had affected her. I appreciated that so much. She then called me five weeks after his death. I was yearning for someone to commiserate with me. We quickly made our way back into each other's arms and lives, and she made me an offer that I couldn't refuse.

She told me that I could move into their spare bedroom for as long as I needed. She would take care of me, make me the comfort food (namely mac 'n' cheese) that I thought Nana would have made for me, and there would be a family around me (a sweet husband and two kids) so that I wouldn't be alone. I immediately accepted her offer. It was a tremendous expression of empathy on her part and a true gift from God. She was my angel and talked me down from a lot of crazy thoughts and feelings. I stayed with them 3-1/2 weeks. I brought my dog, Baxter, and even moved my cats in a week or so later, without their permission. I was afraid they would say 'No' if I asked, and I just had to have my animal family around me. They never said a word, although my cats were not part of the original deal. Michele dealt with the pet allergies, covered up their beautiful couch with a white sheet, respected that my needs were greater than hers, and tried to ignore the fact that my critters were taking over their home.

I helped out with the kids' homework a little and took them to school a few times. This made me feel like I was of some help and not just burdening them, which was good for me. They built me up and uplifted me as much as possible. When I moved back to my house, I felt a bit more stable. My time at their home had been a blessing and a lifesaver. God knew just what I needed and provided.

CHAPTER ELEVEN:
RENOVATION

"I vow to become better, not bitter."

Early in my recovery, I noted that the world doesn't stop for grieving people. Friends would tell me, "You're looking real good, Deb. You're so strong." Yet, I was walking around with a huge black hole in my heart that they couldn't see. I wanted them to identify with it, but they couldn't know how tortured I felt. I trudged through my days, but my life was so empty without Bob. I had been like a child with him. He showered attention on me and loved to listen to me and laugh with me. We had fun together and shared the same wacky sense of humor. He had been my best friend for 15 years and now -- nothing. I talked a lot to anyone who would listen – my therapist, friends, strangers in parks. The decision I had made at the very beginning of the nightmare, to not silence my grief, was turning out to be the best decision thus far. I further decided to never lie about the cause of Bob's death (even to men I would date), and to strive not to be ashamed. I made a decision to move toward health – to become better, not bitter. I didn't want to hate men; I didn't want to be ruined by what Bob had done.

The first part of renovating my life directly involved the renovation of my home. If I could regain some sense of security in the home where Bob had shot himself, I felt I could start to move on with my life. I first had to make the decision whether I could even stay there. Initially, I wanted to move although I had absolutely no energy to do so. On the other end of the spectrum, I also hated the idea that Bob, by his actions, could rip away from me the one place that I had always felt safe – my own home. My friend, Debra, said something to me that I never forgot: "Healing begins at home." I wasn't sure about that, and thought that maybe that was true only if one wasn't dealing with a suicide. I spoke with many friends of varying opinions, and most thought it was not a good idea to stay. Michele felt that I hadn't found any other place that I felt a connection with as much as my own home. She was right about that. I looked at a condo, a rental home, a home to purchase, and apartments in the first six months after Bob's death. I ended up "going with my gut", trusting my own instincts, and learning that only I would ultimately know what I could handle.

The few sparse things I had brought into the living room from other areas in the house were starting to bother me. Initially, I used the living room to process my grief and "talk" to Bob. I would go over to the corner where he died and pretend that I was holding his hand. We always loved to hold hands, and I regretted not running to him and holding his hand one last time while I still could. When I found him, there was a lot of blood on his face and around him. I think I knew that, if I got too close, I would be destroyed, not able to handle what I saw. I believe you know subconsciously what is impossible for you, what will push you over the edge. But, it haunted me that I didn't hold his hand one last time; I even asked the mortuary if I could do that before the cremation. They agreed to allow this, but I decided against it. I couldn't allow the torment of forcing myself to see the same gray skin that had disturbed me so much on finding him dead. But, I punished myself for many months over this decision. I agonized whether I was a good wife. I was also guilt-ridden over the relief I experienced about him being gone. I later read in a suicide book that this is a normal feeling based on the fact we are living under severe tension which is finally relieved when your loved one dies.

My living room still looked empty. After four months, I couldn't take it anymore and decided to rent furniture, until I could hire a decorator who would help me to create a home which would reflect my own tastes. The renovation project took on a life of its own; it was an integral part of the beginning stages of my recovery. I decided on a look that I had always loved. This gave me a new sense of freedom, that this part of my life would be more about whom I was, a place where I would create new memories. I had lived long in Bob's shadow, pushing myself down, and it felt good to start peeking out from under it!

My home needed to reflect warmth and be welcoming and cozy for this part of my life. I wanted to eventually entertain my old friends (and new ones) in a place that felt good. I chose warm colors – the jewel tones – hunter green, dark blue, watermelon, and burgundy to capture a classic country style. This was a masculine look, yet even this was appropriate. I didn't want to deny that I missed Bob's masculine presence, but the touches were distinctly 'Debbie'. Birdhouses were added to create a more whimsical feel.

There was an important link happening, the renovation project in my home to the renovation taking place in my heart. The more together my home became, the more together I felt. I knew I had a long way to go to feel safe in the world again, but this was an important beginning.

CHAPTER TWELVE:
THE SEARCH FOR SANITY

Promise yourself to become so strong that nothing can disturb your peace of mind.

One of the first things I noticed about my recovery was the lack of concentration I experienced. I read in a book about suicide loss that this was typical of suicide survivors. The book likened it to not being able to protect yourself from an unexpected and shattering blow to the head. That is exactly what it felt like – I was shaken, scattered, confused, and unable to focus. I felt absolutely crazy on the inside of myself, but I was so relieved to read that this was normal for a victim of suicide. I was very concerned for my mental health, but to learn that other people had suffered with the EXACT symptoms I was going through was of tremendous help to me.

I desperately wanted my life back to normal. For about the first year after Bob died, I could hardly watch TV. It took about six months to even be able to watch a comedy, and then I would only watch one show per night. I couldn't handle the extra voice in my home, even though I lived alone. I needed so much quiet because of what was going on in my screaming head. Friends' and strangers' opinions about suicide, God's hand in this act, what I would do next to recover, where I would go, whom I would visit, when I could work, how long I could hold out financially, my future, my desperate desire for a sex life, if I could and ever would remarry – AAGGGHHH! These issues were just a few of the things that kept knocking around in my already overloaded brain.

I eventually went to movies with friends and, invariably, there would be a FedEx courier or truck in it. The reminder would reduce me to tears. Sometimes, there would be a sad ending in which someone could have done something differently and the old, familiar refrain of "If I'd only…" would penetrate my head again. I fell apart on Michele in my car after one of those movies because of the things I didn't do differently. I was still tortured.

I listened to very soft music much of the time, meditation tapes, waterfalls and ocean waves. Sometimes, I would be able to listen to upbeat music, latin or disco. I wanted to just let loose and have a little fun. The penetrating beat would help me drown out all the stuff going on inside of me, and "rocking out", even for a short time, was a great and uplifting distraction.

CHAPTER THIRTEEN:
BLOOD ON MY HANDS

I continued seeing my therapist, Cynthia. This was extremely valuable to me and I felt very comfortable talking to her; Bob had even seen her for a few visits before his death. She had requested that he give our gun to me, and he told her that he had. She had also suffered because she hadn't called to confirm this with me.

One day at home, he asked me why I couldn't do better by him and I just broke apart, telling him that I was doing the best I could. Cynthia relayed to me, in no uncertain terms, that Bob had discussed this with her and really knew how hard I had tried to help him. She told me that Bob was very clear on that point and this was a great comfort in helping to diminish my severe guilt.

I had said things to hurt him, things that should never have been said. When I started going to Al-Anon, my anger about the turn our lives had taken started breaking forth and I spewed this anger onto him. The analysis of my wretched life had begun and I was targeting Bob, looking for someone else to blame. One day in the car on the way up to his parents' house, I told him that I didn't think I ever loved him, that I was too young when I married him and it was because I needed him, not loved him. He was crushed. He looked me in the eye and said slowly, "It sure has been a long life." He asked me why he always picked the wrong girl. Less than a month later, he was dead by his own hand.

I remembered those comments I made within days after he died and I raged on the inside about my unbridled mouth. MY GOD, my mind screamed, I KILLED HIM! I knew he was fragile, so vulnerable, and I let loose on him anyway. It would take a very long time to forgive myself for that one action. I believed for many years that was the remark that pushed him over the edge.

I actively sought many sources to help me with this. I didn't know if I could live with the knowledge of MY part in Bob's death. Old friends were invaluable in reminding me that Bob had been suicidal at least five years before I ever met him. Books assured me that suicide is mainly caused by mental illness (especially depression). Mental health professionals assured me that suicide is ALWAYS a person's own choice, that NO ONE ELSE can make someone kill or not kill himself. New age people told me that I had made some kind of a silent pact with him at the beginning that would include the lessons of the years spent with him, as well as the lessons of his suicide. On some level, I knew that Bob had been in trouble with problems that I hadn't created. But forgiveness of myself was not soon in coming.

My mind, body and soul raged with this guilt for years. If only I had known then the One who would wipe my slate clean and enable me to live with serenity.

CHAPTER FOURTEEN:
SORDID SEX

One of the hardest and most extreme side effects of my grief process was that I couldn't get sexually under control. I became massively horny immediately.

Within weeks after Bob's death, I started looking at men's ring fingers in stores, and my mind obsessed with having someone to make love with. I was in dire need from fifteen years of a nearly celibate relationship. Not only were my emotions a wreck, but I was in bad shape physically. Fifty pounds of excess weight, with an ankle that I limped through life with, and a body that so desperately wanted sex was making life impossible.

I was on the phone periodically with a man I'll call Peter, one of Bob's best friends. He was going to be in California on a business trip in December, just 3-1/2 months after the suicide. Friends teased me and said, "Maybe he will be the one to relieve you of your horniness. He's single; you're single..." I was not attracted to him that way, but I wondered if I would have sex with him when I offered him my loft room for the weekend he would be in town. I had shared with him on the phone my great pain over being sexually needy for so many years. He had been separated for some time, as well, and had not been intimate with anyone.

Peter had a college degree in Psychology and he had known Bob since long before the suicide, so he became a key person in my recovery. Bob and Peter had met in New York around the age of sixteen. My long-distance conversations with Peter helped tremendously during the first few months of mental processing because he reminded me that Bob had been suicidal at age 21. Bob had shared with me years before that he felt unloved and wanted to take his life as a young man, but he didn't have the 'courage' to pull the trigger. Peter reminded me of this fact, and that Bob had been in dire straits YEARS before I met him. This was invaluable to me, because my brain was in such a fog. He shared with me the many dynamics and issues he knew about from having known Bob so long, and I was so grateful for the inside scoop. It lifted some of the pressure off me.

I ended up sleeping with Peter and becoming overly obsessed about him and the sex he offered me. I wanted desperately for someone to love me and it was awesome to feel like a woman again. I bought sexy underwear and lingerie. I daydreamed about sex constantly. Even in church, I couldn't get sex off my mind.

I was out of control on the inside and needed to believe that a man would be attracted to me, and would want to make passionate love with me. I was also healthy enough to realize that I was placing too much emphasis on this affair, and that he probably wouldn't be the man I would marry. Peter felt the pressure, too. I jumped in head over heels and took a dive right into him as my next savior. Peter helped me to drown out my grief for a short time. At that time, I was so desperate that I would have spent any amount of money to get constant sex and companionship. The balance lie in the fact that he lived out of state and had a good job to maintain, so our relationship could only be as intense as our letters, phone calls, and occasional visits would allow.

Our shared sexual passion had seemed harmless, but after only a little over a month into our relationship, I would again be thrown for a loop. A young man had violated me when I was 19, and it had remained with me for years. Peter knew about this experience and repeated it. I returned home to California after that trip, shocked and shaken by his insensitivity and upset by the level of trust I had placed in him. I believe it was his way of getting me off his back and it worked. I was devastated, once again.

My loneliness was profound and unbearable. Bob and I always shared a wonderful camaraderie with each other, and I missed that connection from the depth of my soul. We never grew tired of talking with each other. We had a care and concern for one another, and a genuine heart for each other's well-being that had stabilized me for over 15 years. With that shattered and no one to take his place, I started responding to personal ads in an effort to find Mr. Right, or at least, a compatible physical relationship. I knew this was crazy – what I really wanted was to be married again, safe in someone's arms who really knew me and loved me.

I talked for hours to strange men on the telephone. I met some of them over drinks or dinner and slept with most of the men I met. Several were living with women. One had just broken up with his long-time, live-in love. One was a one-night stand that left me feeling used, although I held myself responsible for the invitation into my home and body. One had agreed to an open marriage with his wife, and was ready for sex as long as he used a condom. He was seeking a "spiritual" connection, which made what we were doing seem more acceptable. The only problem was I didn't feel beautiful or spiritual in our connection. The truth was that he had a woman he had committed to, the mother of his two children, waiting at home for him. One man was married and his wife didn't know about me. Another man was newly separated and totally not ready for a desperate, needy woman.

One man after another passed through my life, a virtual revolving door of empty and sordid sex. It was sick and I knew it; I just hoped one of these men would be the one who would rescue me from my mess of a life. What kept me repeating this behavior was the feeling I got from having a man on top of me, chest to chest. It was the feeling of being covered, contained. I wanted to feel safe and secure again, and their body strength seemed to provide it, if only for a short time.

Having sex felt great, but only while I was in bed. It would hit me afterwards that I wasn't experiencing intimacy and beauty; I was giving up so much of myself to people who didn't love or appreciate me. I always had to be talking to at least one man. More often than not, I had several on the horn at the same time. I knew that this was crazy and futile. I knew that what I was doing was wrong, especially with the married men. I had a good moral compass for right and wrong, but I tried to ignore it. Some of my friends even convinced me to just get what I needed at the time, to throw out the rule books and have fun with it, even if it was from married men. But, deep down it wasn't fun. Cynthia and I discussed in one of our sessions the decision to sleep with people who belong to someone else, and how those choices impacted me.

My pervasive unmet physical needs ruled for many months. I operated on AutoPilot, controlled by my intense sexuality and robotically doing what felt best. The only thing that saved me was my guilty conscience. After one or two sexual encounters with each man, I would snap back into reality and stop sleeping with them. But, my behavior was not without detriment. The threat of physical danger with men I barely knew, as well as the possibility of AIDS or venereal disease, was always lurking because I didn't always insist on using a condom. I had interviewed all these men thoroughly, but the truth is that any one of them could have done serious damage to me. Through that whole time, however, I sensed that I was being protected, that God was watching over me and would not let anyone hurt me permanently.

I jokingly called the personal ads "the loser hotline". The fact that I was on the other end of that hotline didn't escape me, which made me one of the losers. I also knew that I had the potential for something better, purer, inside me, and that my behavior was at least partially a reaction to the raw deal I'd been dealt. I read books during this time that stressed personal responsibility, so I didn't stay in that frame of mind for long. At the same time I was behaving like this, I was looking for a way out of it. Not satisfied to just excuse it, I was searching for a better way of life.

Cynthia was concerned that this was no longer my way of getting my long-term physical needs satisfied, but that it was a psychological need. She told me that this constant search for a man wasn't good for my self-esteem. I knew she was right. And there was something else. I just knew that the wholeness I wanted to live with, the peace of mind I so desperately was seeking, the unconditional love that I longed for, would not be found in another person. My friend, Gay, mentioned Jesus as being the 'peace that surpasses all understanding'. I was intrigued because I had such little peace. I believed that the void I felt was more about not knowing who God was than about being lonely for Bob or needy for another man. Only a relationship with the One who could love me the way I couldn't love myself was the true answer.

CHAPTER FIFTEEN:
HANGING ONTO...NOTHING

My tears formed a pillow for my heart to rest upon.

Nine months after Bob's suicide, I still wasn't doing well. I cried endlessly; my tears just wouldn't dry up. It was like Bob's suicide had broken open all the other pain in my childhood and life that had long awaited healing. I seemed to be trying to purge the most painful moments of my life from my body. That felt good, to finally be able to express the deep sadness I always felt, but it was also wearing on my body. The process was difficult, to completely mourn not just one traumatic loss but try to heal your entire life. It was the most incredibly exhausting time of my life, and I wondered how much more I could take. My fatigue and depression were starting to overwhelm me, but I didn't feel ready to go out into the world yet, try to find a job after years of being home, and be subjected to the world's cruelties on top of my own grief process. So, I stuck with it, read and learned as much as I could to help myself. But my friends were starting to get concerned that I was prolonging this process, and there was a nagging doubt in me that I would even be able to get to the root of all my pain.

The worst part of this stage of the recovery was that I lacked any sense of personal safety whatsoever. I felt like I was just hanging in the air, my feet suspended but anxiously moving and trying to find some foundation, something firm to stand on. Instead, I found nothing to hang onto.

I had read about a grief recovery program that held workshops about an hour from my home. I called and spoke to one of the facilitators and he was great. He deeply identified with what I had been going through, even the sexual issues.

When he found out there hadn't been much physical intimacy in my marriage, he said, "Then there must be this sexual energy flying....going to your crotch, your boobs, everywhere." I burst into tears instantly. He had put into words exactly what I was going through. I signed up to attend the weekend workshop being held the next month. I hoped that I would finally be able to gain some real answers to my problems.

The workshop was valuable in the information shared. It offered a different way of looking at my losses. I sat next to an older gentleman who had lost two wives to suicide. I didn't miss the "coincidence"; I didn't feel it was one. God had brought him to the workshop all the way from Florida to sit next to me. He wasn't even going to come to that workshop, but his family was having a reunion and he flew in for it. We consoled each other and he was the one I most closely connected with.

I learned how to write about and try to release each loss I had experienced. I liked to write and the class taught me to look at each relationship in its entirety – the good and bad – in an effort to release it and move on. However, there was something that I questioned the first day of the workshop. The facilitator said that people would tell him, "Jesus will heal me" and he responded, "Jesus can't do it". I thought that was pretty arrogant, that he would feel his program was more powerful than Jesus was. It didn't sit right with me.

Returning home, I initially felt relieved and energized, as if I had found a panacea for all my problems. I felt actively involved in my healing process, which gave me some sense of control over my life. I continued to delve into and work my grief out with a man who attended the workshop with me. He made the hour's drive to my house and I fell apart in his arms after each one of our "sessions". It felt good to be in his arms and he was sensitive in his treatment of me. But, a gnawing sense of no real resolution and a low-lying depression remained, and I realized that these exercises were only a band-aid.

My grief partner told me about a hypnotherapist he had seen in La Jolla, who had a great reputation and credentials. I was still seeing my talk therapist, but decided to try hypnotherapy at the same time. I was attempting to dig out the roots of my pain, instead of healing only the suicide. I thought thorough self-examination was the answer, and that relentlessly combing over every area of my life would result in inner wholeness.

The hypnotherapist took a thorough history of me. He thought I would need from eight to twelve sessions with him, and I readily agreed to them. Although expensive, I wanted to feel good again. The chairs were cozy, the doctor sympathetic, the "turn your thinking around" tapes relaxing, and the dream analysis particularly interesting. After eleven sessions, I was slightly relieved and a little more aware of the ill effects of alcoholism on my life. But, there was nothing of major proportion in this treatment that could wipe out the kind of intense emotional pain that still resided in me on a daily basis.

I started to realize that I was spending an awful lot of money to find something that would help me to be able to deal with life functionally. I was thankful I had the money, but so far, I hadn't come up with anything that could touch the core of me. I would keep on searching, fighting the good fight, and determining not to be destroyed by one person's actions.

What I really needed was a Great Physician who could and would heal me totally, completely.

CHAPTER SIXTEEN:
A "RAY" OF HOPE

By the spring following Bob's death, I decided to host another foreign exchange student, a 15-year-old French Canadian girl from Montreal. I selected her because of the wacky picture she sent along with her profile. She was decked out in a sheer white, two- piece midriff outfit with crushed soda cans all over it. This appeared to be a costume, and I thought it was really funny and imaginative. I thought that she would be a delight to have in my home. We also had the same birthday, exactly 20 years apart, which I felt was a sure sign that she was "meant to be" my next guest.

Veronique stayed with me that summer for 22 days. We had an awesome time together, and I took her everywhere she wanted to go. We went to Hollywood, Beverly Hills, and around L.A. on a stars' home tour. We went to the beach a couple times and to the mountains horseback riding. We had a slumber party with a bunch of the other girls from the program, which was a God gift in itself to have those bundles of energy in my home! She spoke English very well and we were interested in the same things. We discussed psychology and philosophy of life, our heart's desires, God, her country's government, family, Bob's suicide, friendship, and men. She was such a wonderful girl that I decided I would visit her in Quebec for our mutual birthday 2-1/2 months later. I had been planning a bicycling trip through Vermont with Michele, and Montreal was only an hour's flight away from the states.

Veronique and I had such fun adventures together! I was still on the "loser hotline" talking to men, but I didn't sleep with anyone during her stay. Caring for her and going places with her balanced my life out. I was still pushing through life due to low energy, but I loved having her with me. Close to the one-year anniversary of Bob's death, I decided to host a celebration for making it through the first year. Most of my good friends arrived for a backyard get-together. I wrote a speech including each one of them, extolling my appreciation and thanking them for what they had done for me. I thought things were improving, and I was so desperate for the next year to be uplifting. But, I was still rounding up men on the loser hotline, trying to convince myself that it was okay when it wasn't.

As my Vermont biking trip neared, I could not get myself under control. I started to unravel and thought something terrible was going to happen. I had handwritten a will. Feeling broken and unsure of what was going on, I had a serious conversation on the phone with a caseworker from a mental health hotline late one night. She strongly advised not going on the trip, but I didn't feel like I could disappoint Michele by canceling the trip that we had been planning for 9 months. Suicide recovery has severe ebbs and flows, but this breakdown seemed to come from out of the blue.

I talked to Cynthia about it and she advised that, if I insisted on going, Michele and I could try to be "containers" for one another. I could help with her fear of flying and she could try to help with my flailing emotions. The trip ended up being a combination of fun and disaster. We experienced glorious countryside, viewing exquisite, multi-colored trees in their splendor during fall foliage season. It was a joy to both of our souls; Michele and I both felt that we were in God's country. God was revealing Himself to us through creation.

But, I was carrying much unresolved anger inside me toward Michele and my past medical experiences from my car accident. I unleashed on her one night at the dinner table in front of the other people we were on tour with. I demeaned her, where she worked, and the doctors she worked with. It was ugly. We didn't talk about it afterwards or resolve it; there was just this black cloud hanging over our relationship.

I was very fatigued through most of the trip and trying to cycle the 20-35 daily miles was too much for me. I felt like I was having a nervous breakdown. By the time I reached Montreal, I had never been so tired. I moved through the next four days with Veronique's family as best I could, but I couldn't wait to get home to my animals. I had been gone a total of thirteen days, probably ten days too long. I found, through these failed attempts to lead a normal life, that I would not be able to handle what was once so simple. I longed for what I had known in the past; my new lesson was to honor where I was, and to do the best I could managing smaller things. Suicide had dramatically changed my life, whether I liked it or not.

I still couldn't find anyone to share my life or have sex with. I wanted so badly to be in love again. I felt like I had so much to give and no one to give it to. I had started dating a man nine years my junior from the loser hotline. His name was Ray, and he was a devout Catholic virgin. He was a very nice man, although considerably less worldly than I was. He was still living at home with his parents and hadn't experienced being out on his own yet. He seemed overly innocent for the age of 27 and most of all, he wouldn't give me what I most wanted, which was sex. Thoughts of wild passionate sex were still controlling me. I lamented over this, unsure of what to do with myself.

One night, he agreed to follow me into my bedroom. He told me to lie down on the bed on my tummy and he would give me a massage fully dressed. This sounded good, and I thought I could coerce him into making love with me once he started. Instead, he gently touched my eyelids, face, hair, back, arms and legs (avoiding my derriere), and I will never forget how respectful and loving he was. I tried to seduce him, but he didn't let me. I didn't understand what was happening at the time; I just knew there was something different about him and the LEVEL of love and care he showed me that night.

He was my "Ray" of hope. He treated me like a precious lady who was worth respect. God will send people into your life to reflect Himself. Through Ray, he showed me how much He would love me, if I would just give Him the chance.

CHAPTER SEVENTEEN:
SUITABLE SUBSTITUTION?

I had shared many things about my life with my grief partner, Kirk, both in grief work and on the telephone, and he had opened up parts of his life to me. He was soothing to my soul; he listened to my outpouring of pain and the ways I was trying to grow through each of my life experiences. He knew about my sexual issues and teased that if I gave him a chance, he would "give it to me" for at least 45 minutes. With my various lovers, sex never lasted long enough, I couldn't get filled enough, and the sordidness of my sex life with men who barely knew me made it not beautiful enough. I continued this pattern for some time even though it never gave me "enough". I thought that, if I sowed my wild oats long enough, I could get it out of my system, but the opposite was true. The sex was empty and unfulfilling, yet my desire for it increased.

As I grew closer to Kirk, I called my grief counselor who had facilitated the program and asked what he thought about the idea of dating my grief partner. He stayed neutral and didn't advise whether to date him or not. He told me that we were two people who had expressed truth to one another and that could be the basis for a relationship.

My better judgment was telling me that my reasons for dating Kirk were all wrong. I went back and forth with my soul-searching, but my loins were still controlling me after sixteen months of widowhood. We moved into sex immediately, on our first date. I gave him much bodily attention; he abided by his promise to "give it to me" at least 45 minutes. It felt secure to have someone who was reliable, who would go places with me, and who liked spending time together. We saw each other on the weekends, and on most Thursday nights when he came to my house after work. We ate home-cooked meals by candlelight, and sometimes a fire, and it felt like being married again. I loved that and I felt calmer than I had since the suicide.

I wanted to get on with my life and enjoy a true boyfriend/girlfriend relationship. However, during this time, my foot doctor and I were discussing that I was a perfect candidate for a revolutionary new ankle joint implant operation. He was the only doctor in California and one of a handful of doctors nationwide performing this type of surgery, and he had great confidence in the operation and what it would do for me by taking away my arthritis and allowing me to walk easier. I discussed it with Kirk, along with my frustrations about being under the knife again and the long recovery period. He encouraged me to have the surgery anyway, even though we were new to dating each other. So less than one month into our dating life, I was off my feet again, enduring yet another surgery, along with another round of physical therapy, Jacuzzi treatments, and theraband exercises. Kirk stood by me, sent flowers and visited me in the hospital. I appreciated having him in my life during this difficult time.

However, there were many problems with our communications. I tried to overlook them because it felt good to be getting regular and lengthier sex, and to have a man in my life was such a relief. We were a complete mismatch in so many areas of life, however, that I knew at the 3-month mark, it wasn't going to last. I tried to break up with him at that point, but I was too insecure to let him go. We continued to see each other and try to work it out.

We moved through the summer with each other with difficulty. I entered into an emotional release program recommended to me by Jim, another physical therapist friend. He had gone through the program and made significant changes with his life. So, although the program was very expensive, I decided to once again bite the bullet, spend the money, and give something new a try.

It was a grueling program, physically, mentally, and emotionally. It was referred to as marathon group therapy, but it was more like shock therapy spread over eight days, designed to move you quickly through the process of knowing exactly how you sabotage your life and the limitations you place on yourself. There were pages upon pages of written homework, sleep deprivation, diet and other controls – an extreme regimen that I liked to call 'gestapo tactics'. I felt like I was in the military, but I was willing to go through it to get to the bottom of my problems in life and heal from the suicide.

I left the program on an extreme emotional high because of what I thought I had gained – some sense of how to turn my life around. This was short-lived, however, because I didn't know how to process all the negative information I learned about my life. It was traumatic to deal with the after-effects of knowing everything wrong about yourself, yet not having an effective way to deal with it once leaving the program. What I most needed was to be saved from my life, my thinking, and my wrong choices. This program advertised true transformation, and I had been optimistic, but it was mind-boggling and frustrating as I sought these changes in my life. I worked hard, giving 150% of myself both in the program and in the fifteen months of follow-up meetings, in my repetitive quest for wholeness. But, I was starting to get the sense that I really couldn't help myself, that it would take something much greater than me to change my life. I had done everything I could, moving through the program and sessions with fierce determination and a focused intensity on self-improvement. As I continued in this vein, my world became blacker and more depressing. It was horrifying because I had first come out of the program extremely joyful, with a euphoria that I had never before experienced. I thought it would last, but when I came crashing down from that high, it was a hard fall.

Kirk had also put himself through the emotional release program just a few months after me, but I was so miserable in the relationship to begin with, and there were no lasting changes that would make it a success. I tried around the 7-month mark of our relationship to break up with him. Again, it didn't happen. I couldn't let go of him out of my fear of sheer loneliness and a heavy desire for continued sex. I felt trapped. I knew what it was like to spend month after long month without a man, and I didn't want to do it again. However, I continued to learn about personal responsibility and that awareness led me to know that I had made a wrong decision for the wrong reasons from the start. When I finally accepted my part, I broke up with Kirk after nine months of dating. I felt a little stronger to handle it, and I had arrived at the conclusion that it was far worse to be in a bad relationship than with no man at all.

I returned the diamond necklace to him that he had given me for my birthday the week before. With my girlfriend, Linda, in tow, I went to J.C. Penney and found a pretty cubic zirconia necklace to replace it. I was proud of myself. It would mean being alone again, but that was okay. I respected my courage and I was on my way to becoming whole.

CHAPTER EIGHTEEN:
DEAD IN THE WATER

Within days of breaking up with Kirk, Michele broke up with me. She left a book she had borrowed in my mailbox with a letter stating that she didn't want our friendship to continue. She felt slighted that I had become so attached to my new program friends, and she was right in her assessment of the situation. I wrote her a note stating I would never forget how she came through for me like no other after Bob's death.

Within days, I had lost two of my biggest support systems. It was 26 months into the suicide recovery, and I felt more lost and alone than ever before.

I kept trying to convince myself (and others) that I didn't miss Kirk, but I was dreadfully lonely. I acted fanatically by calling him, then hanging up quickly when he answered. Although I knew we were wrong for each other, the sinking feeling that I was once again alone hit me hard. The initial elation I had felt at the time of our breakup diminished and the loneliness set in quickly. To make matters worse, I had to deal with seeing him at our group functions and it was very uncomfortable.

I missed the sex more than anything, the physical closeness we had shared. I missed his arms around me. I was tortured when I had to see him at our friends' Christmas party. More than ever, I wanted to beg him to come home with me that night, to make love with me again, to not leave me. My body and emotions were screaming for him. With a force outside myself (God) giving me the strength, I miraculously didn't ask him to come back. Instead, I went home and cried hard into my pillow for hours, until sleep finally overtook my fatigued body.

I felt abandoned. I had no family to cling to, I still hadn't found God in the whole mess, and I was so sexually needy once again. Michele, the friend who had been closest to me for two years, was gone. I moved through the next few months in a daze, eager to get on with my life, but not knowing what to do next. My depression was overwhelming, as I moved through days of not caring too much about anything.

I felt like a drowned woman, with no help or hope in sight.

CHAPTER NINETEEN:
HEADING "HOME"

It had been a hard Christmas season without being able to go to Michele's or her in-laws' home. With no family of my own, spending the holidays with them had been stability for me that I relied upon each year since Bob had died.

I had continued to talk to people about God, get their opinions, see what they felt I should do next, and determine what I should read. Many people had come to my door in over two years from different churches. I talked to people in parks about God. I really wanted an end to my long search for truth. It didn't escape me that the more stable people were connected to Jesus Christ, but I still refused having a Savior. I wanted to have control over my own life – that was all there was to it. I had lived 37 years to achieve that. I had been controlled much of my life, and I didn't want to be owned by anyone. It was also obvious to me that my desire to control my own life was not moving me toward any sense of peace or fulfillment. Instead, I remained in the depths of despair.

There was a man that came to my door just a few months after Bob's death. I told him I was happy with my New Thought church (when I was) and that I wasn't ready to make a change. He was understanding and said something to me that I never forgot -- he hoped that I would grow in deeper relationship with God there. I thanked him for his sentiments, but something struck me about those words. I thought about them from time to time over the years. I knew I wouldn't grow deeper at my church. The more philosophies I studied (some eastern religion included), the more confused I became as to what path was right. Could all paths be right? Did every road lead to God, to heaven?

At one of my first church workshops, we were asked to make a drawing. Folding our sheet of paper into four quadrants, we drew a flower, a tree, a road, a mountain, a snake, and some other things. On the right corner, I drew two paths – one was narrow, the other broad. We were told later that corner of the paper was the spiritual quadrant. I wondered what the significance was in two roads so vastly different from each other.

I went to a New Age store after Christmas and saw a flyer extending the invitation to usher in the New Year at a retreat with an "enlightened being". It wasn't nearly as expensive as everything else I had tried. Maybe she could shed light on what path I was to take. The idea of spending time with a guru certainly sounded interesting. And it was going to be a new year, a new adventure, and hopefully, a chance for a new life.

They advised me to bring a journal and a special picture or memento to lay on their altar, a token representing who or what I worshipped. I was taken back by that; I didn't really worship anything. I had tried to meditate, to slow my brain down and be mindful, as the Buddhists suggested. I liked some of the tenets of Buddhism, because my mind had raced so badly since Bob died. I was still desperate for peace, but had a very difficult time with meditation. I had been such a fast mover through my life, a workaholic with an intense need to accomplish and achieve my goals. I moved through life by my mental processes. I was extremely logical and analytical, so 'becoming still' was nearly impossible.

I had bought two green heart-shaped stones and tried to pray with them. It didn't work for me; I was praying to the air. There was no relationship, no connection. It seemed futile. I tried to envision God being a white light, as my friend, Annecia had suggested, but that wasn't personal enough for me. I needed God to be REAL.

There were about twenty people at the guru's house, some of whom lived and worked there. They seemed really nice. There was an array of items on the altar. Most of the people brought pictures of East Indian gods or prophets. It was a bit eerie. Once again, I was where beliefs were all over the place and what I most wanted was certainty, not further scattering.

We journaled, talked with and massaged each other, and ate lunch while this "enlightened being" was praying in her bedroom. We were told we would get to see her that evening. We sat around in a circle on the floor and chanted odd-sounding words. I didn't feel comfortable chanting "Om nama shiva" without knowing what it meant. So as not to cause speculation, I chanted with the thought that I had asked God for the truth of Him and prayed that He would not let me go until I had it. This had been my continual desire since shortly after Bob died, and I hoped that God would read my heart.

We were told to shut our eyes, but I opened them long enough to see this very nice-looking blonde woman in a long, flowery tie-dyed hippie dress slink into the room. She addressed the people in the group and asked them why they were there. It seemed that almost everyone knew her already. When she got to me, I don't remember exactly what I said except to tell her where I was at in life. I mentioned Bob's suicide, and her piercing blue eyes infiltrated me as she clutched her chest and said, "God's got me." Sensing I was to follow her lead, I clutched my own chest and repeated, "God's got me." She smiled at me in the most loving way. I liked her and smiled back, but something felt weird. She came up to me later and said that she knew me. She had never met me, so I presumed she meant that she felt an inner connection with me.

I noticed the people at the retreat bowed to her and to each other and someone told me that it meant, 'The god in me accepts the god in you.' We had formed a circle outside later that night in front of a bonfire and were requested to say a prayer that was meaningful to us. I used a prayer from my New Thought church that we repeated at the end of each service. I was standing next to the guru, holding hands with her. She turned to me and told me that I belonged with them now. If I had been any weaker of a person, I would have probably moved in right then. I desperately wanted to belong somewhere. But there was something terribly wrong with what I felt was going on there. I kept my eyes open and observed everything closely. I did not believe they had the truth about God, and was not at all convinced that I belonged there.

The next day, I had interesting conversations with some of the attendees. They told me they thought my 'suicide story' was too fresh, like it had recently happened instead of being a 28-month-old event. I heard one of the girls scream as she rushed up a hill, and it was explained that she was doing some kind of release work. We talked about rebirthing, but I was convinced that nothing I had done in 28 months for myself even remotely resembled being born again. I had heard enough mumbo jumbo in the paths I had experimented with. I was more than disgusted with the self-help treatments and rituals that led nowhere. I wanted to believe God was in me like they told me, but I neither felt it nor believed it. There had to be more.

I wanted to leave early on the last day, but was heavily persuaded by one of the men who worked there to stay and "work through" my feelings by journaling them. I did as I was told, but I found no point in it. I missed my animals and I felt there was no longer any reason to stay.

The people had been overly friendly to me, but I hadn't found the true God I had so longed for. I just wanted to go home -- to my cute little house with my sweet animals and to find answers that would lead me Home to the real God.

CHAPTER TWENTY:
BELONGING TO MY BELOVED

"Life's most painful losses can lead to life's most beautiful findings."

- Rusty Berkus

I was glad to be home. I decided to just go with the flow, rest, read, and enjoy my animals.

After the hectic Christmas season, January was a 'down' month for the craft shows I was working, and I was tired of trying so hard to make everything work in my life anyway. I hadn't succeeded in anything – my little business, finding the real God, or my relationships. I just wanted to relax, take care of myself, eat healthy, homemade food, sit by the fireplace, and read. I was at a loss as to how to help myself. It was two years and 4-1/2 months after Bob's suicide and I was still hanging.

I started to read a book someone had recommended to me, and it felt good not to be pushing myself for a change. I had moved swiftly into my recovery process, exploring every which way to heal, and I had relentlessly pressed on, even when I needed rest. I didn't know how long I would need to recover from my "recovery process", but I was dog-tired. This was the first time since Bob had died that I really "let go". I was tired of thinking. I didn't want to think about my finances, my spiritual life, my home, my work…I just wanted rest. And it felt right to honor that. I needed replenishment.

A few days into my relaxation time, a Yosemite Water salesman by the name of Jerome knocked on my door. I took an instant liking to him and we started talking. I told him about my life after Bob's suicide, that I felt I was being led, and that God had been watching over me. He said, "You seem to be searching." I agreed and we talked further.

Jerome asked me some questions about my belief system. My spiritual beliefs were mainly made up of other men's truths expressed in New Age books, ideas about God that I felt comfortable with, philosophies which suited my personality and that I wanted God to approve of. I had no solid facts, just a conglomeration of my own and other people's opinions. I told him I thought we all had divine light in us from the beginning, a belief I had absorbed from my New Thought church. He asked me what I felt about sin and separation. I had just spent days at the retreat listening to a song called, "We have never been separated from You." I told him that I didn't believe in sin and the separation that he thought it caused from God, and that God was loving and kind toward us. I spilled my mixed bag of beliefs out onto him as he listened intently.

With authority, over the next hour and a half, he shared with me the real truth about God. He told me that there is sin in us and that it does separate us from God. When I balked at this, he used an illustration about kids – their inherent selfishness and how easily they lie, verbally and physically hurt each other. He told me we are all born into sin and that sin is easily recognized, even in very small children. I argued with him and asked him if his kids didn't lie because they felt anxiety that he and his wife were creating, feeling that they had to protect themselves. I didn't spend a whole lot of time around children and didn't have my own, but I was sticking strongly to my viewpoints. He said he never taught his kids to lie, but that they do automatically. He told me that our sin does separate us from God, because He is so holy. His standard is too high for us to attain on our own, so God provided His very own son, Jesus, to be sacrificed for our sins. He told me that God's Word states, "The wages of sin is death." That really struck me hard. It seemed so punishing, so violent, more than I wanted to bear at the time. I only wanted God to be loving, but Jerome was teaching me that there was another side to God – He was also just. But, instead of punishing us, He loved us so much that He didn't spare His own son, to take on our punishment, give us peace, and connect us with Him. I liked that part a lot; I wanted to believe God loved me, wanted me to be home with Him, and would choose me as His own.

I had tried so hard all my life to be a good person, hoping all my good deeds would one day satisfy God and that I would <u>feel</u> that I was pleasing and acceptable to Him. But, I never felt any closeness. It was maddening to go through life, striving to do the right thing, making the right decisions, doing good, giving myself away, only to feel that it was all futile and that God's wrath was on me. I had done wrong things, too. I thought about my own sin – I had lied, manipulated and hurt people, said filthy words, and felt vengeful toward people who had hurt me, among other things. I killed my own baby at the age of 19 through an abortion. I said terrible things to Bob and other people, things that hurt their heart. I didn't want to take a long look at it, but the truth was in front of me. Before he left, while at my door, I asked him what he thought I should do next (as I had every other church member), and what he thought I should read. He told me simply, "The Book of John" in the Bible. No one had ever said that to me.

I pulled out the study Bible I had bought for Bob and started reading the Book of John. I read a chapter or two at a time, then contemplated what I was reading. I had been scared of the Bible, but this time was very different. I left it open on my coffee table, so that I would return to it and finish.

God gave me complete quiet time. It was very unusual that my phone didn't ring. No one stopped by; no one was trying to reach me. I was absolutely drawn to each chapter and I had complete understanding as I read. My doorbell didn't ring but, at some point over those three days, someone from a local church left off a little pamphlet at my doorstep. I picked it up and started reading more about sin. On the back, there was a prayer to repeat if I wanted to be connected to the real God, if I wanted a real relationship, and didn't want to be separated any more. I thought of how I had worked so hard my whole life to be someone whom He would be proud of, yet all the striving in my own strength had done me no good. I had wound up fretful, anxious, and exhausted. I pondered this really deeply. I had gone down and analyzed every other path available to me, every program, every book, every movement that I thought would connect me, and nothing had worked. When I really believed that I was a sinner, from my heart, and that nothing I could do in my own efforts had or would connect me to God, I read that prayer on my couch.

I had asked God to not let go of me until I found the truth of Him. As I read through the pages of the Book of John, Jesus revealed to me the truth of Himself and I was finally able to receive Him into my heart. He had been faithful to me and had never let go of me during my search, just like I asked. There were parts of this gospel that pierced my heart and brought me such joy. In one profound moment, He revealed, "I will not leave you as orphans; I will come to you." This was singularly the best news I had ever heard. I had been left an orphan in the world. So many people had deserted me, but not Jesus.

I learned that "He was in the world and, though the world was made through Him, the world did not recognize Him. He came to that which was His own, but His own did not receive Him. Yet to all who received Him, to those who believed in His name, He gave the RIGHT to become children of God – children born not of natural descent, nor of human decision or a husband's will, but born of God." (John 1:10-13)

Jesus said, "For the one whom God has sent speaks the words of God...The Father loves the Son and has placed everything in His hands. Whoever believes in the Son has eternal life, but whoever rejects the Son will not see life, for God's wrath remains on Him." (John 3:34-36). And finally, "We will come and make our home with you." As important as my home was to me, it had been a desolate place without the Father and the Son residing with me. He told me that, "No one can come to me unless the Father who sent me draws him". He said in His own words, "You did not choose me, but I chose you." His words were beautiful and many were prefaced with, "I tell you the truth...". I could understand why He is called the Good Shepherd. I knew in that instant the truth of Him, that He had laid down His life for me.

I had set up a sacred space in my bedroom a few months before, to go to in those times of extreme darkness, and maybe find God, talk to Him in a way where He would finally hear me, in a way where I would finally feel connected. With my own power, it hadn't happened.

But God's power is different; it is the power of His Holy Spirit. As I neared the end of the Book of John, I knew, with peace in my heart, that this was the truth about God that I had sought. All my life, my soul had been empty; there was a missing piece to my puzzle. I brought my Bible into my sacred space on the floor, opened the door to my sacred cabinet, lit a candle, poured out my heart once again....and He listened. With complete honesty, I begged Jesus to be my Savior, told Him how badly I needed Him, and that I couldn't do it alone any more through this life. I told Him I wasn't sure if He heard me the first time on the couch. I expressed my desperation for Him.

It was in that moment that I physically felt like a two-ton weight was lifting off me. The word that kept going through my head was "RELIEF...finally RELIEF." I burst into tears, knowing that my long search was over. As I continued to cry my heart out, I felt like the top of my head came off and bright light was pouring into it. I had never felt anything like that, and I couldn't move. I didn't want to move; I wanted to sit still for it. I was experiencing His most overwhelming, irresistible LOVE for me, and I was blissful for the first time in my life. Light seemed to filter into my body and I sensed Jesus' presence in my body and around me, in my bedroom. His Holy Spirit filled me up, and gave me the wholeness I had been seeking. I thanked him for ending my search. I had been getting so tired with the endless search for Him. I kept thinking, "The search is over, the search is over, I'm so glad the search is over. I finally found You."

My friend, Gay, had given me a video from her church and exhausted, I lay on the bed to watch it. Jesus was bringing the people who believed in Him into His kingdom. Not everyone was entering into His presence, only the ones who believed in His name for eternal life. Every time He brought someone to Himself, His arms would go up, as if to welcome them, and I would quickly move out of bed and put my hands on top of His hands on the TV set. I wanted to identify with Him and, if I could have jumped into the TV set to be right in His body and close to His heart, I would have. I told Him I loved Him for what He had just given me, a real connection. I wanted to be closer to Him. I belonged to Him, and it was good…this peace I had always longed for, but couldn't find in any other way, on any other path.

Heavenly peace is what it was. I could now live, and sleep, in heavenly peace.

Things which once were wild alarms
Cannot now disturb my rest,
Closed in everlasting arms,

Pillowed on the loving breast,
Oh, to lie forever here,
Doubt and care and self-resign,
As He whispers in my ear,
I am His and He is mine.

I had memorized this poem years before. I finally knew what it meant.

CHAPTER TWENTY-ONE:
DOING THE 'WORK'

When I left the emotional release program, I thought I had all the tools I would need to 'do the work' which would garner me a better life. I thought, 'Finally, a way to be free…transformed!' This was not to be the case.

It was suggested that I hug myself and speak into a mirror repeatedly that I loved myself. I continued for many months with this hugging "work", hoping to be able to feel the love for myself. The nights I spent on the floor in my living room feeling lost and abandoned are too numerous to mention, but I continued to cling to myself. I was desperate for connection, purpose, and a permanent steadying of my nerves and gut. I never got it. You see, I didn't love myself then and no amount of hugging or affirmations would make it so.

I was also advised to continue getting the anger out of my system. For many months, I verbally bashed my most hurtful abusers, clubbing a pillow, ripping into a big cardboard picture I had drawn of them. I scared the heck out of my animals with all this rigmarole! One night, in front of a full-length mirror, I turned on myself and screamed "I HATE YOU!" with such power and force, and about the most evil face I have ever conjured up. That was my most disengaging moment – I was shocked that all my "work" had come to that. When I revealed it at my group session, it was lightly brushed aside with, "Now, we're supposed to be living in the light." I wish I had known this one truth: That which we dwell on increases. I was a fiery, hateful ball of rage by the time the Lord saved me and led me away from this so-called "therapy". Amazingly enough, I came to the Lord, received Jesus in my heart, and was baptized into my new life during my last 8 months with the group – AND STILL DIDN'T QUIT THE

PROGRAM! One day, during a particularly happy time, the facilitator remarked that I was getting clearer. I pondered why that would be. All the "work" that I had done in that program and the many months of follow-up sessions had not given me the clarity I had so yearned for. The only recent difference had been that Jesus Christ had entered my heart, and was making the internal changes. I walked away from the group sessions and made a run toward true emotional, mental and spiritual health. It was timely and perfect, as is all God's decisions.

For years, I had been advised to "honor myself" so I spent a lot of money traveling near and far, going to amusement and water parks, redecorating my home, and buying things for myself. But the emptiness continued. Temporarily, it all felt good. But trips and pretty purchases do not fill the size of hole I was enduring in my heart.

What I am most trying to convey is that the world's solutions are not God's. He tells us, "My ways are not your ways. My thoughts are higher than your thoughts." These therapies are what the world knows and recommends, but they are not the answers that He has for us. I believe that He wouldn't have wanted me to endure the continual emotional havoc I was experiencing, but I was too stubborn to listen to a Savior. The self-awareness I had learned had been valuable, but these teachings were a detriment to my already unstable nerves. All teachings not of the true God ultimately fail.

However, it was not a waste. God ended up using my tumultuous path, in future conversations I would have with suffering people, in planting seeds so that they could come to know Jesus, and most certainly in the writing of this book. But in hindsight (being 20/20 as it is), if I had known then what I know now, I would have saved myself the time, trouble, tears, and terrible turmoil that being on a path outside of Jesus creates.

You see, the nights were too dark, too lonely, too fearful, too much for me to bear for too long. God knew this and saved me as quickly as possible. I praise God that He plucked me off that curvy road and placed me onto His safe, sure, straight path. I pray the same for you.

Having personally experienced the many roads that can be taken but which do not lead Home, I believe the Lord is inspiring me to make this known so that you may know the one road that does lead home to Him. I think back to my drawing of the two roads, one broad and one narrow. Jesus says, "Broad is the road that leads to destruction, but narrow is the road that leads to life, and few will find it. I am the Way, the Truth, and the Life. No one comes to the Father except through Me." (John 14:6) Yes, indeed. He is the Way home to God in heaven, the Truth about God, and the Life inside those who will receive Him into their hearts.

There was one huge positive to 'doing the work' to the extreme with which I took it. It broke me down enough to where I realized all that work wasn't "working". In fact, it is a barrier to the work God would do to straighten your life out. Sometimes, I revert back to a works mentality, based on years of habit. But largely, I try to remember that my life runs smoother and things work best when I let Him work out all the issues. This doesn't take the responsibility for my life off me. I am just a willing partner with the One who created me, Who knows the deepest desires of my heart, and how to best accomplish His perfect purpose for my life. My choices are better because of the One who guides me. This kind of life brings something I needed for a long time – ease and sanity. And, He has been much gentler on me than I ever was on myself.

Yes, His work actually works! We don't have to be busily burrowing out our sins on the futile road to self-improvement. That calls for a Hallelujah! Jesus tells us, "Come to Me, all you who are weary and heavily burdened, and I will give you rest. Take My yoke upon you and learn from Me. For My yoke is easy and My burden is light." Amen.

CHAPTER TWENTY-TWO:
SEALED WITH A CROSS

The seeking heart finds at journey's end,
Jesus as its closest friend.

- Roy Lessin

Within months after inviting the Lord into my heart, I placed a picture of Jesus praying in my sacred cabinet. I started going there daily to share my thoughts and feelings with Him. His presence was palpable as He listened to me, assuaging my fears, and comforting the very center of my soul. I finally knew the peace of Jesus that I had longed for, the "peace that surpasses all understanding" that Gay spoke of right after Bob died.

One night before my quiet time with Him, I was straightening up my room and listening to a CD mixed with songs from different artists. I finished and sat down early in front of my sacred cabinet. I left on the CD, although I wasn't sure why. I normally would put on meditation music or nothing at all for my time with the Lord. Instead, I sat down and finished listening to a Kenny G saxophone piece. Immediately following was a Luther Vandross song. I lit my candle, illuminating Jesus' face, pondering the greatest Love of my life, and contemplating what He had done for me. It was then that the words of the song penetrated me, how His love is all I'd ever need, that I vowed to be one with Thee and how my pledge of love felt so right, and, especially, how nothing could take our love away.

I began to sing this song every day to Jesus, over and over. Although written to be a love song meant for a man and woman, I was falling in love more and more with Jesus, and singing to my Firstlove. His was the only love I needed above all others. He had created me, molded me and shaped me, placed special qualities inside me, knew me and loved me better and more intimately than anyone else ever could. He had followed me, waiting 37 years for me to return fully to His heart. It's hard to describe the level of love that flowed out of me during this time. I was absorbing so much of Jesus' love for me that my strong desire was to share it right back with Him.

One day, after spending time with the Lord in my sacred space, the doorbell rang and there was a stranger at my door, a girl who needed to use my phone as her car had broken down. I had just come out of my long devotional time and the minute I opened the door, she exclaimed, "Oh, you're so beautiful!" I didn't look particularly beautiful that day. I was wearing jeans, no makeup, and my hair wasn't even done yet. What she saw was the Lord's beauty through me.

This was an exquisite time of my life. I felt like I was floating on a cloud. I experienced joy like I'd never known before. Jesus lifted the heaviness of a long, depressing life right off me. I was free…to love Him, to enjoy Him, to learn of Him. This time of my life was so precious to me; I would clutch my chest and want to hold Him there forever. He promised me, "I will not leave you or forsake you." I cherished those words; I treasured that He would never abandon me. In those months, I realized why Jesus is called the Gift. He is God, the Father's precious Gift to anyone who will receive Him. Accepting this free Gift into your heart brings assurance of His never-ending presence and the abundance of inner life like you've never known.

Kirk had given me a country music tape by Alison Krause with a song on it called "Palm of Your Hands." After I was saved, I listened to it repeatedly in my car. I would sing to Jesus as I was driving down the road, most fervently about being in the palm of His hands and how His grace was providing for me.

His grace was absolutely permeating my life. My faith in Him, given to me by Him, enabled me to see right through the tragic circumstances of Bob's suicide and how God's grace had provided for me all along. It was His kindness toward me that had ultimately led to my repentance. When all the events of my life had lined up with His perfect timing, He had led me right to His Son.

I brought many of my varied feelings to the Lord during this very special time. I had a wall plaque that read, "God will heal your broken heart if you will give him all the pieces." I passed by that plaque for months until one day, I asked myself: What pieces are you not giving Him? I realized that I still carried tremendous anger over Bob's suicide, hurt about my childhood, questions that haunted me.

That night, I took those questions and intense feelings to the Lord. I sat down in my sacred space and poured my guts out. I was raging, but real with God. I wanted to know why Bob had killed himself, why I had to have the unstable childhood, why He would place me in an alcoholic family, why, why, why....Everything I could think of that I felt destroyed by, I gave to Him that night. And He answered me. He gave me a moment where I knew, beyond the shadow of a doubt, that everything that had ever happened to me had been perfect because it was all for the purpose of leading me home to Him. He had to have me back in His arms again. He loved me so much that He couldn't let me go. It was a light bulb moment. I was blessed with that one moment in time where I knew, with complete understanding, that my Father had been watching my whole life and divinely orchestrating events He wanted to happen, combined with the events that He would rather not have seen happen, so that I would one day run to Him. Everything

HAD to happen exactly as it did for this one HUGE purpose...to be back with Him, reconciled to His heart.

Nothing else in life means as much as this. To know Jesus and to love Him and to have those answers means everything. Author Max Lucado has written, "Answer the large question of life, and all the smaller questions fall into place." All the years of wanting to know who I am, why I was placed here at this time, the significance, meaning and purpose for my existence on this earth, those many small questions had been answered by answering the one big question: Who is God?

CHAPTER TWENTY-THREE:
SOAKED IN THE BLESSINGS OF GOD

Nearly six months into my walk with Christ, I started intensely desiring baptism. Jesus' love had moved me and I wanted to take the next step with Him. As is often the way with the Lord, He put several people in my path that had just recently been baptized. I would ask them about their baptism, and their eager, positive responses made me want it even more.

It was summertime and my world was getting warmer. A few months before, I had attended the Easter service at the church of my friend's husband, Dan, who was the minister in a church out of town. I had experienced a terrible longing and void in my heart for the past twelve or thirteen years on Easter. The first time this happened, I had to leave a friend's home and celebration, and take a long walk with Bob around the block. I started hyperventilating and didn't understand what was going on with me. For years, I had tried to analyze why that particular holiday was so hard for me. There wasn't a link back to any bad family Easters. One Easter just before Bob died, I was walking in a local park and watching families play basketball together. I asked myself if I was longing for a better family, but I knew it was something much deeper. Easter 1997, the puzzle pieces finally fit together. Easter is the day celebrating His resurrection, and I had longed for Jesus to be resurrected in my heart. There was a void in my heart that only He could fill. My heart was finally at peace and I could now enjoy every Easter holiday.

I talked to Dan after the service and he loaned me books to learn more about Jesus. I was a bit ungrounded and not sure where to attend church in my town, how to proceed ahead in my new life. Dan was a dear man and answered the many tough questions I posed to him about Christianity. It was evident that the Lord had saved my soul, but I still had much to learn. I didn't want to get baptized in the faith without being clear on my decision.

I had never wanted to use Jesus as a crutch. I had been suffering for years before I came to Him. I was sure that I needed a relationship with a real Lord, not just to use Jesus to make me feel better because I had been in despair. I didn't want to get baptized in the faith without more knowledge of its meaning. My life had certainly improved a hundredfold; I just had to make sure I was of right heart.

My doubt, fears and questions were in the forefront. I struggled with many issues. I was assured that Christ had already taken the punishment for my sins on the cross – that His sacrifice was perfect, so that I did not have to be. My sins – past, present and future – had been forgiven so completely that God couldn't even remember them.

I thought back to my guilty existence without Him. I had carried so much burden for my transgressions in life, and blamed myself for 37 years for things which were not even my fault. Knowing how deeply His forgiveness ran through my life is what propelled me toward my baptism. I was obviously loved – He had proven that to me. Jesus had given me the RIGHT to become a child of God; it had been a miracle of His grace that I was no longer able to resist His love on that January evening. God's wrath was forever off me and His joy was on me. I read and learned more about Him, counseled with Dan, searched my own heart, and thought I was ready.

Shortly before the big day, I dealt with one last dilemma in my mind. As I was relaxing in the bathtub one night, it hit me like a ton of bricks that Christ claims to be the ONLY way to God. I had been so tolerant of all paths to God, believed that truth was different for different people, and that each person had to make his own individual decision on what path was right for him. I got out of the bathtub, torn about this, wondering if I would become rigid and judgmental now that I was Christian. I immediately went into my sacred space and poured my heart out, telling the Lord my feelings and how conflicted I was. Was He really the ONLY way to God? I immediately got my answer: "I am the Way, the Truth, and the Life." He had proven that in His relationship with me. My heart had not known a moment's peace without the presence of Jesus. I knew, without a doubt, that I was making a commitment that was not only right for me, but that was right for everybody else, anyone that would give Him a chance to penetrate their heart. Jesus is the Truth, and the Truth shall set you free. I had experienced this freedom in my body, in my heart, the very center of my soul. I didn't just believe in Him; I knew Him.

The 3-year anniversary of Bob's death was quickly approaching and I asked Dan if it would be inappropriate to make August 22nd, the anniversary of Bob's suicide, the day of my baptism. He said that there was nothing positive for me in the suicide and told me that we could make that day mean something else. I loved that the day could be remembered as a day of beauty instead of tragedy. Jesus had found me in the wake of the suicide, and that was the most positive thing that could ever have come from it.

I wanted the day to be so meaningful and the Lord knew it. The Lord knows you so intimately, He knows the desires of your heart even before you speak them out. I wanted to be baptized in a special, significant place. I thought about various locales, some quite a distance from me, and Dan said he would go anywhere I wanted. In the meantime, I had started attending a church I felt led to and my pastor there recommended inviting my friends. I had wanted my baptism to be private (me, God and the minister), but he helped me to understand that baptism is an outward and public demonstration of an inward change.

Then, God gave me the thought...Menifee Lakes, the lakeside community not far from my house, where I had bicycled, walked my dog, and fed the ducks. I had experienced many "moments" there. I would sit under trees, stare at the lake, and cry violently, uncontrollably, wondering where God was, and how He would make my life right. I had pleaded with Him to make Himself known, where I could actually feel His presence. This didn't happen, of course, until the night I humbled myself before Him, confessed my grave need for Him, and invited Jesus into my heart. I decided that the lake where I had spent so much time in my grief should be where I would enter into my baptism.

There was only one problem...it was a private lake and I didn't live there. I phoned and spoke with a man named Don, the lake manager, to see if he would let me use it. I explained everything to him, so that he would know how important it was that my baptism be held there. He told me that there was nobody allowed in the lake, but that I could use the swimming pool at the Beach & Swim Club. I had seen it and loved it. It looked very natural, like a beach, and appealed to me greatly. Surprisingly enough, I didn't book it then, but he said it was available for that day. In the meantime, I thought of other places around the ocean, but nothing seemed as perfect as Menifee Lakes. I started putting together my guest list. About a week before the ceremony, I realized I hadn't placed the final reservation on Menifee Lakes, and hurriedly called Don again. I was sick to my stomach that I had waited so long to reserve it, and praying that I hadn't botched my chances of having the ceremony there. Don told me that he had never taken me off his calendar. God is so good, even when I am absent-minded!

I was now free to extend invitations. I wanted the ceremony to be personal, and I didn't know anyone yet from my new church. I decided that the people present should be the friends who had helped me tremendously with either the suicide or in my spiritual life. My special day was coming up quickly, and that turned out to be perfect. Since time was short, I called each friend to let them know of my new relationship with the Lord and why I wanted them there. I told each one what they had done for me or said to me that had made a difference in my life. Many were surprised and didn't remember saying anything profound! But, I had absorbed their wise words, so it was very important to me that they know why I wanted them to attend. There was about 15 of us, an intimate number for an intimate ceremony, which was the desire of my heart.

The important morning finally arrived, and I got up and immediately journaled my feelings for the special occasion. It felt like a wedding day, so I wrote:

This day, I will marry my best friend, the one I laugh with, live for, love...

This saying was from a glass heart I had given Bob on our first anniversary. I felt that my baptism day was more special than any earthly wedding could be, for I was marrying my Lord and Savior.

I then went into my sacred space. I had my Bible with me and opened to a devotional page where a Christian woman had written about her father dying when she was only twelve years old. She had read through the Bible cover to cover, in an effort to understand why God had allowed that to happen, why God hadn't protected him, and what would become of her life. She finally decided to turn toward God instead of away from Him and told Him, "If you will be my Father, God, I will be your child." I was so touched by her questions and struggles. I repeated that line to my Heavenly Father and used it as my own request. There was reference to a scripture chapter and verse, so I thumbed through the pages to reach Psalm 68:5. It read:

A Father to the fatherless,
A defender of widows,
Is God in His holy dwelling.

The dual meaning of that passage broke my heart open. I had never had a real father, but a succession of stepdads. And, of course, I was a widow, who, in my worst of times, had needed serious defense. I praised Him for how special this day was already becoming...that He would offer that particular passage on my special day delighted my heart. The words sung to my soul, as I realized that I would no longer have to be fatherless, and that He had defended me in my widowhood when I was barely aware of Him. I cried for some time with sheer joy and pleasure. The gift of this scripture shouldn't have surprised me; God had revealed His preciousness to me before. But this day, getting that passage from Him was extra special and He knew what it would mean to my heart. I thanked him profusely, over and over again.

I left 30 minutes early for Menifee Lakes to read a poem I had written for God to Him. It was called 'Full Circle' and detailed the circuitous path I had taken before He took hold of me. I found a spot on the grass close to where I would be baptized, then shared my feelings about the day. I asked Him to accept my poem as a love offering. I started to read it, looking up at the sky and enjoying His creation.

I hadn't read very much before a beautiful Golden Retriever distracted me. I tried to get back to the poem, but I couldn't. I kept staring and smiling at him, but I didn't know why. The lady who was walking him said, "So, you're taking a break, huh?" I told her I was just about to be baptized and that

I'd come early to read my poem to God. She stopped dead in her tracks and said, "Are you Debbie?" Then I knew who she was. I ran to her and we hugged tightly, embracing each other as long lost friends.

I had met Sue two years earlier at the lake, shortly after my grief recovery program. She was sitting on a bench with her beautiful dog by her side. Although not intending to stop there, I sat down on the bench next to her, with Baxter by my side, and she opened up her sad life to me. Her husband had just had an affair with her best friend and she was broken-hearted. I told her what I had learned in grief recovery, but it didn't seem like enough. Finally, I told her that we weren't meant to hurt needlessly and that God would not waste our suffering. I didn't know God at all, didn't know Jesus at the time, but I just couldn't believe that we were going through all that darkness for nothing. We talked quite a while that day, then exchanged phone numbers, but neither one of us followed up. I didn't know that she had ended up in a church parking lot shortly after. She had run to the altar to be saved by Jesus in this community church. We were now sisters in the Lord.

She told me that I was part of her testimony and called me "her angel". I had not known that God had used me to speak to her, before I even came to know Him. It was an extra special delight of my day to be reconciled to her. I asked her if she would like to come to my baptism and she heartily agreed. I was amazed that I hadn't seen her at ANY TIME in that whole two years I had been constantly around the lake. God had saved our reunion for my special day.

I needed a resident of the lake to pay the small fee for the baptism for me, as all transactions needed to be handled through people who lived there. I asked the husband of a friend, but he was unavailable. I then thought of George, a man I had worked for on a temporary basis for a few months. He said he would send his wife, Vicky, to meet me at the Beach & Swim Club. Sue laughingly told me she could be my backup, if for some reason Vicky wasn't there. God was working out all the details and I was basking in His care.

My other guests started to arrive, as well as Vicky and their daughter, Alex. When Dan arrived, I excitedly told him what had happened that morning with the psalm the Lord had led me to. Dan listened closely, then showed me His Bible. He had his bookmark on the same page to read Psalm 68:5. God was showering me with one blessing after another!

Dan shared beautiful scriptures from the Bible with us, then told everyone what an important day it was for me "because Debbie gains a Father today." That really struck my heart. If I had ever had an earthly father, this probably wouldn't have been such an important moment. I had always wondered who my real father was. I had been illegitimate and never knew him, but I had tried to locate him, and I thought about him a lot through my whole life. It was another one of those unanswered questions. I realized that never again would I have to be fatherless, and the moment was overpowering. Dan then did something that I will never forget. He said that we say, "How much do You love me?" And Jesus said, "This much." Dan stretched out his arms wide, saying, "Then He stretched out His arms and died." It was quite an illustration, and I clutched my heart at the thought of what Jesus had endured for me on the cross.

We went into the pool and I suddenly became scared. I know now that I was afraid of losing control of my life. I didn't realize that I would never have to be afraid of His authority. I had not been blessed with good authority figures in my life. But, God had given me Jesus, who is the only One who can control you without destroying you, who has your best interests at heart at all times.

I repeated a prayer after Dan, then he immersed me. When I was completely covered with water, he brought me up again. Once again, I felt huge relief. I let out an indescribable grunting sound – more burdensome load taken off me. I had a big smile on my face, and I heard my friends applauding. I exited the pool, to be greeted by my friend, Joi, who was holding the white robe I'd bought for the occasion. Dan had teased me when he saw the Victoria's Secret bag it came in. It was the only place I could find a suitable white terry cloth robe!

Afterwards, Dan told me to enjoy being soaked in the blessings of God! He told me that I would decide how far to go with God, at what level I would live in Him. I signed a certificate and the big 'Bank of Heaven' check that was created just for me, made payable to Debbie Wilson. In the memo part, it read: Remember I love you! In the currency section, it read 'God's Son: The Life of Jesus Christ'. Jesus had to pay for me to gain entrance to the Kingdom of Heaven. I endorsed the back of the check and to this day, it's still an important reminder that the Kingdom of Heaven is mine!

I cradled each of my guests' heads as I hugged them. I felt so loving toward them, as Jesus had loved me. I could tell everyone had been moved by the experience. God had used my writings, as well as Dan's own touches and special Bible verses, to tug at each person's heart. Vicky and Alex were supposed to leave after the payment was made, but ended up staying for the whole ceremony. It was wonderful to see the Lord using my baptism to touch other people's lives.

Three days later, I saw Vicky and Alex in the Christian bookstore. I knew their witness of God's love at my baptism had drawn them, and that He would use my life in a positive way. The love Jesus and I shared with each other would transfer to the people around me. He would use me to touch hearts as He had touched mine.

It was an extraordinary moment when I came to realize this. I picked up a little pamphlet called "Born to be a Blessing." My life would indeed be a blessing, a gift back to Him for all that He'd given me.

CHAPTER TWENTY-FOUR:
EPIPHANY

Close to my second birthday in the Lord, I was bothered by the fact that I wasn't growing spiritually as quickly as I would have liked and, sometimes, I wondered if I was even saved. I had moved away from God's grace and, as a dog returns to its vomit, started sleeping with Peter again. I was distressed by this and desired to completely live in God's joy and peace again. The Lord started to reveal to me His perfect design for my life. I was reminded that He jealously loves me and that I am His jewel. Through this depth of love for me, I started to understand that He guards me, seeing to it that nothing gets in the way of our love for each other. Working in my heart, over a period of time, He strengthened me to move away from Peter and a few other people who were destructive to my walk with Him.

Having experienced God's great love over my life, I remembered the tremendously high moments in my first years with the Lord. As I was contemplating this one morning, I went to my gratitude journal where I had made an entry the night I was born again. I had written: The Book of John; My prayer to Jesus, "getting it". I sat down on my couch and asked the Lord if He remembered the night I begged for Him on the floor of my bedroom. A warm feeling flooded me as I recalled how beautiful that night was - the feeling of light and relief, His presence around me, and all the events leading up to that wondrous day. I thought to myself, 'What an epiphany that was'. I rarely use that word and wondered if it meant awakening. I had a very old, worn, 10-year-old dictionary on my desk. When I looked up the word, it didn't show epiphany starting with a small 'e', but a capital 'E'. I read the definition: A Christian festival (January 6) commemorating the revealing of Jesus as the Christ to the Gentiles. I stared at the definition and date in utter amazement. The entry in my gratitude journal reflected that Jesus had revealed Himself to me as the Christ on January 6th.

What is most incredible about this is that I am a "date" person. I have a photographic memory when it comes to special occasions. I remember the birth dates of people I worked with 20 years ago. As everything comes from Him, God had placed this quality in me at birth. Then, God had allowed all the events of my life to work together so that I would receive Him into my heart that January 6th. My friend, Judye, told me that it could have been the 5th or 7th but in His perfect timing, He made sure that it was January 6th. Knowing what this revelation would mean to me on a day when I felt shaky in my faith, He placed a trait in me at birth that would play a major part in a precious moment that we would share together in the future.

He does this repeatedly with me. He never fails to meet me right where I'm at emotionally. He knows me intimately, He knows the number of hairs on my head, and He knows I'm into "dates". I've had so many things like this happen since I came to the Lord that I know it's not coincidence. Even with my hardheaded nature, He makes it impossible to deny these events as being directly from Him.

CHAPTER TWENTY-FIVE:
THE HURT HEALER

"I bathed you with water and washed the blood from you and put ointments on you" (Ezekiel 16:6)

No one goes through life unscathed, my friend, Patty, once told me. The Lord has begun my healing process, and He will continue with it until the day Jesus returns. This takes a great load off me! It is He who is faithful to complete the work. There have been many issues to bring before Him -- abandonment, rejection, relationships, self-loathing, sexuality, and anger, to name a few of the bigger ones. I am still under construction. There is, however, one thing I know for sure: The Great Physician takes each hurt and deals lovingly with me, applying His healing balm.

One day, I was reading a book about damaged emotions. There was a story shared about a woman whose father had abandoned her and her mother hadn't wanted her either. This woman's therapy assignment was to meditate on the question: Where was God at the moment of your conception? After three days, a prayer welled up in her and she wrote a letter to God, which, in part, included these words:

"Knowing the pain in store for me, You gave me a mind to pull above the hurt until, in Your own timing, You could heal me. You were there when my mother gave birth to me, looking on in tenderness, standing in the vacant place of my father."

Had abortions been more prevalent in the 1950's, my mother told me I would have been one. I suffered hearing those words, and lived a life of self-loathing, low worth and self-esteem. If my own mother didn't want me, then why was I even here? What purpose was there in bringing me into the world? I grappled with this my whole life and, even after I was saved, it hurt me. The woman's prayer in the book totally hit home in my heart. As often happens, the Lord immediately brought to my remembrance a psalm that tells how we are created and His hand in our existence. I thought it was Psalm 119. My Bible lying beside me, I picked it up and opened it, placing it on my lap. It had fallen open naturally to Psalm 139. As I gazed at the words, it was the psalm that God had laid on my brain. I read:

"For You created my inmost being,
You knit me together in my mother's womb;
I praise You because I am awesomely and wonderfully made.
Your works are wonderful; I know that full well.
My frame was not hidden from You
when I was made in the secret place,
When I was woven together in the depths of the earth,
Your eyes saw my unformed body."

The dawning realization struck me that my mother may not have wanted me, but the Lord did. I pondered this great truth and held it closely in my heart. I spent many hours that day, thanking Him, crying into Him, and allowing Him to cleanse my system of the words that had broken me many years before.

God knew whose womb I would be placed into, He knew what I would have to go through, and He knew when I would run to the foot of the cross due to the lifetime of hurts that I had taken on. He knew what I gave to my mother and what she gave to me, and how that relationship would make us who we are today. And He knew that I would be His child above all. He deals with each issue as it surfaces, through my prayer time, reading the Bible and other books, and in relationships with others. I praised Him for the glorious way that He revealed these truths to me. I read Psalm 139 again and again, and repeated, "Your works are wonderful; I know that full well."

That was one of the most precious days I've spent as I grasped the truth of who I am in Him. There is a saying that God doesn't make garbage, but I had felt like garbage. He showed me that day, in a most dramatic way, the truth about myself.

I go to Him as every hurt surfaces. He never turns me away. He has always handled me carefully and sweetly. I know that He not only loves me, but that He is in love with me. His open arms are always available for me to move into them. He has comforted me like no other.

As He heals my hurts, He recycles them and sends me out into the world to help hurting people. This is ultimately the reason for suffering – to return to the Lord, receive His healing, and then allow God to use our lives for other hurting people.

I have shared so many profound experiences with the Lord, they are too numerous to mention. I continue to write down each major experience with Him, but I would run out of paper if I journaled all the small details of my life that God has involved Himself in.

For years, I was blinded, unable to capture or feel any movement from God. I thought it wasn't possible for me to be religious or spiritual. Now, I know that it is completely within His power to turn on anyone's spiritual light. He's a personal God, actively pursuing a relationship with anyone who will be open to receiving His Son. He has proven Himself to be what I thought I could never have – a very real Lord of my life.

CHAPTER TWENTY-SIX:
LIFEBLOOD

"Deliver me from bloodguilt, Oh God"

There is no denying that I felt Bob's blood on my hands for a very long time. My profound feelings of guilt broke my spirit. Although I am completely aware that no one can make a person end his or her life, I know that I played a part in Bob's decision. I can freely admit this now, because of Whom I've confessed it to in the past.

One sorrowful night years ago, I poured my guts out to the Lord of my great pain over the things I had said and done, and the things I had not said and done, with regard to Bob's suicide. I knew that my salvation in the Lord had freed me of all my sins – past, present, and future. But, I felt pulled toward sharing with Jesus just how badly I felt about my comments and actions. Through what seemed like endless tears, I spewed out my anguish, the torture my heart had carried. Jesus bore those wounds on Himself, forgave me, and massaged my wracked and weary soul.

It was nearly impossible to accept and receive Jesus' great love for me because it involved blood. Blood had been a real negative for me, in Bob's suicide and in general throughout my life. I couldn't watch bloody gore in the movies or on television. I found it violent and gross. When Nurse Kandi told me that Jesus died for me, shedding blood, it was a revolting thought, representing brutality, suffering, and death. I angrily shot back, "Who asked Him to?!" Bob had died in his blood and it had been horrifying for me to witness. What made Jesus' blood different?

Jesus' blood is born of love, God's love for His children. He tells us, "For God so loved the world that He gave His one and only Son, that whoever believes in Him shall not perish but have everlasting life" (John 3:16). So, who asked Jesus to shed blood for me? God did. And Jesus willingly went to the cross for you and me. As Max Lucado puts it, "Jesus would rather go to hell for you than go to heaven without you."

The blood Bob shed nearly destroyed me. The blood Jesus shed for me on the cross freed me from the blood Bob shed.

God knows and, deep down, we know that we need to be saved from ourselves. No one can admit to being sin-free. As human beings, we've lied, deceived, manipulated, harbored wrong thoughts and feelings, and worse. God is so holy that we cannot enter into His presence without payment for that sin. We are separated from Him because of it and, with our sin, comes a price that someone needs to pay. It will be us, if not Jesus. Without Jesus, on Judgment day, I would have been standing before God giving an account of everything I did in my lifetime. My deepest shame and personal horror has stemmed from murdering my baby and my murderous tongue with respect to Bob's suicide. Nothing is hidden before God, and these things would have been unveiled. Mercifully, I won't have to explain. Jesus took the punishment for me on the cross, and He will reveal me as 100% clean to my Heavenly Father on that day. "The punishment that brought us peace was upon Him, and by His wounds, we are healed" (Isaiah 53:5). What a joy and a blessing to have clean hands – once and for all!

Webster's Dictionary defines the word lifeblood, as "the blood necessary to life; a vital element". Jesus' blood is a vital element to all our lives, not just my own. Won't you consider coming before Him and inviting Him to be your Savior, to bring you near to God through His blood? His blood is the only thing that CAN do that. His blood will bring you peace; He is the Prince of Peace. Won't you ask Him into your heart today so that you can enter into peace with God? He is faithful and has promised to do it if only you will ask. You would say, from your heart:

"Lord Jesus, I need you. I have sinned and fallen short of your glory. Please enter my heart and reconcile me to my Heavenly Father right this moment. I want to be Yours; I don't want to be separated any more. Thank you for dying on the cross for my sins. Show me the way and guide my steps in my new life with You. In Jesus' precious name I pray...Amen."

CHAPTER TWENTY-SEVEN:
A "RIGHT" TURN

Be careful what you stand convinced of...

Several summers ago, I started to take my dog to a park about three miles from my home. This park is within an older housing tract in the area, and I drove Baxter over to let him run around amongst the many trees. After going there repeatedly (nearly every work night for a few weeks), I headed over with him one night for our usual sojourn. I made what I thought were the usual turns to get there, but it was as if the park had been moved! It obviously wasn't where I thought it was, but I was insistent that the park was in the housing tract I had driven to. I spent more time trying to find it, making the same turns onto the same streets to no avail. I became frustrated with myself and the situation as I continued for the next 10 or 15 minutes trying to find the park.

I finally decided to stop the agitation. As I pulled over to the side of the road and quieted myself down, I realized that I was NOT on the proper path to the park or else I would have already found it. Obviously, I needed to break away from what I was doing in order to find the proper path. I looked straight ahead and realized that, if I turned onto the main road and moved out of that area and what I was doing, I might find the park. It was a weird moment because I was SO CERTAIN of the choices I had made to get to my desired destination.

I pulled onto Newport Road and traveled about a mile when I came across a stoplight at Evans Road. Something familiar flashed into my mind as I made the right turn there. I went straight down the street and there was the park at the tail end!

I share this story to convey to you that you can be SO CERTAIN that you are on the right path and not be on the right path at all. If your path to God has not been through Jesus, His Son, then you have made wrong turns and they will not land you at the destination you hope to one day be – namely, heaven.

I liken this "park" experience to my path to God. I, too, took many wrong turns, insistent that I was right. But it was not until I made my "right" turn into Jesus that I found the true God. It was not until I moved away from my old pattern of thinking that I was blessed with a REAL relationship with the living God and the assurance that I will spend eternal life with Him.

You may be at this crossroads yourself. Be careful what you stand convinced of. You may just be on the wrong path and in desperate need of a "right" turn. I pray that you will make that "right" turn toward Jesus today.

CHAPTER TWENTY-EIGHT:
A FAMILY FOR THE LONELY

"Here's to sweet dreams and wishes that come true"

I want to share with you something very near and dear to my heart. As I moved through the years following Bob's death, the saddest issue I had to deal with was that I had no family to belong to, to help me through my toughest moments. I longed for a family that would hold me tight.

When you receive Jesus into your heart, you become a full-fledged member of God's household, God's very own family. My soul rejoices with this truth! Never again will I have to be alone, for I am one of God's own! Psalm 68:6 reveals, "God sets the lonely in families." I have experienced God's restoration in this area, and those times have become the most beautiful of my life.

A few months after my baptism, I decided to sell my home, simplify my life, and rid myself of some of the mental energy it took to maintain an expensive home. I wanted to rent for a while and let someone else handle the upkeep, while I learned more about God and took a rest. My house sold instantly and I had no idea where I would live. I had just started a new job, and was weary and ill. As I lay in bed wondering about my housing dilemma, I heard through a still, small voice, "What about Menifee Lakes?" With a surge of energy and excitement, I felt compelled to drive around that neighborhood. I was pretty sick, so I told God I would give it a half-hour and, if I didn't find anything, I needed to come back home and rest. Within ten minutes after arriving in the community and driving down just a few streets, I found the 'For Rent' sign on a darling, little white home close to a park and gazebo, with an entrance to the lake trail from it. I thought to myself, 'If this is a 2-bedroom and it's as clean on the inside as it is on the outside, I pray it will be mine'.

I called the phone number on the sign and met with Ray, the realtor. It turned out that he lived right next to that park and gazebo, and could come over immediately. The house was a very clean, cozy 2-bedroom with a cute little backyard. Even my furniture would fit perfectly in it! I was concerned about the owner allowing me to rent with three animals, so I prayed about it hard, and God granted my desire. I moved in to the community I had always loved, and it was a joy to be close to "my" lake. Being at Menifee Lakes carried deep meaning for me. It was a joy to my soul; I had come home.

I met and connected with such sweet people (and their dogs!) on my daily walks with Baxter. Ray and his wife, Jean, became my new dog-sitters. Both of my friends that used to watch Baxter when I traveled had moved out of state, so this was a real blessing. Ray and Jean loved and cared for Baxter when I was away, as they did with many other neighborhood dogs, and I could call them to let Baxter out if I was going to be home late. There wasn't a day that went by that I didn't thank God for bringing me there. I sang worship songs on my walks at the lake, rejoiced in God's creation, in nature and with the people around me.

One of the first people I met was a cute kid named Kourtney. She was about about five years old. I learned that her mom, Karen, had been widowed just six weeks after Bob died, and that she had been left with four children to raise. Over the next several years, I got to know her and each of the children very well. My love for them grew and I became an important part of their lives. We have shared such lovely times together. We are connected as family in the Lord. They drew me into their hearts and entwined me into their lives the way real families do.

For years, I had longed for an old-fashioned Christmas. I envisioned a roaring fire, hot chocolate, Christmas carols, simple gifts from the heart, a pretty tree, and lots of love in my home. God granted that desire of my heart Christmas 2000.

Buying $1 tins at an antique store, I filled them with tidbits I wrote to the kids of the special times I had shared with them. I wanted to completely open my heart and tell them how God had used them in my life, and what lovely qualities I felt God had placed in them. I wrote about 5 or 6 special experiences for each child, typed and printed them, then cut each one with scalloped scissors on green and red paper, and put them in the tins. I also gave them little statues I had in my home that reminded me of them, and I made personalized picture keychains that reflected their hobbies and who they are. I received a last minute Christmas bonus, so I bought Karen a massage gift certificate with it. I used brilliantly colored foil wrapping paper, an outer expression of my inner joy! Several friends stopped by with fudge, a gift, and a visit. Money was short, but love was long, and I thoroughly enjoyed the preparations.

With lump in throat, I reveal with supreme gratitude how much the Lord blessed me! When we seek first to honor Him, He honors us. First, my little family picked out a mug from my collection for their hot chocolates. We then held hands and entered into a special prayer in my kitchen. Each of us shared from our hearts, mainly about the meaning of the season, our gratitude for Jesus, and what we meant to each other.

Hot chocolates in hand, we moved over in front of the fireplace toward the glimmering tree, Christmas carols playing on the CD player. I started pulling out presents for the kids. Their eyes wide, they opened their gifts in excitement. Karen asked them to read some of my writings. The looks on their faces told me they were touched by my heartfelt words.

We ended our precious evening, talking about how tender Karen's kids are as a result of not having what others do. Because they lost their dad early on in life, I see great compassion in them for others' sorrows. I shared with Karen that they are who they are because of what they have NOT had. We ended the evening in prayer, and the kids shared with Karen on the way home how much I had spoiled them!

We spent the next night, Christmas Eve, at their Aunt Kerrey's home, filled with warmth, loving people, good cheer, and sweet gifts. Karen and I then went to her house and, after the kids had gone to bed, talked long into the night about the Lord and what He was doing in our lives. At some point, we looked up at the clock and saw that it was about 1:00 a.m., Christmas Day. We locked hands and prayed Jesus' birthday in. It was absolutely perfect, a beautiful way to usher in the day.

The Lord had spoiled me, too.

CHAPTER TWENTY-NINE:
NOW I KNOW WHO TO THANK

Nothing else heals your spirit. As you now know, I tried so many ways -- psychotherapy, hypnotherapy, sex, men, possessions, travel, food, friends, self-help books, grief recovery and emotional release programs, Reiki and body massages, the New Age movement, and a psychic or two thrown in for good measure! The reason why they cannot touch you deeply and heal your life is that they are not truly spiritual, because they are not of the <u>Holy</u> Spirit. They are bandaids for the soul, offering up little "bits" of temporary healing. But the true Healer is Jesus Christ. He is the soothing salve. Having a real relationship with Him means having a real relationship with your Creator Father in heaven. He created the heavens and the earth, everything and everyone, yet we won't accept that He created us for fellowship with Him – the most important thing to Him. Jesus is the only way to gain entrance to God's loving heart, the only way to be redeemed in a world and a body filled with rage, guilt, shame, selfishness, unforgiveness, jealousy, and false pride.

Other philosophies claim to have a grasp on the deep inner man, but the truth is that there is a God-shaped void that exists in each person's heart that can only be filled by Jesus Christ. You may reject this fact, but it doesn't alter the truth. St. Augustine tells us that our hearts are never at rest away from the One who created them.

We try to fill the void in many and varied ways, and those ways will be temporary quick fixes, not permanent solutions. We will come up empty again and again. We have all experienced this. We get a new house, and we're happy – for a time. A new car, and we're happy – for a time. Material possessions, and we're happy – for a time. A new spouse, and we're happy – for a time. We don't have to accept happy – for a time – when we can have God's joy for a lifetime.

Now, I live with the love, peace and joy that I longed for all my life. Now, I know who to thank: Jesus Christ. Good things happened to me before I became a believer in Jesus Christ. But, I never knew who to thank. The world told me to thank myself, so I tried that – A LOT. It was empty, the self-sufficient lie. If it was indeed me making all the good things happen in life, then that meant there was no room for Someone greater than I to be loving me, guiding me, and wanting the best for me. When you realize that it is God creating the beauty of your life, there is far more fulfillment and reward in that than taking the credit for "creating" the good life yourself.

We are lied to in the world in this respect. Set goals! Be all you can be! Be the captain of your ship! Honor yourself! How about honoring the real God instead and what He can do in His power, so much greater than our own? He created us for beauty – for a fulfilling and eternal life -- for inner peace – for true rewards – for what makes life worth living.

I thank Him for that.

CHAPTER THIRTY:
BASED ON A PROMISE

He heals the brokenhearted and binds up their wounds.

I was privileged to hold a friend in grief after the death of his 20-month-old baby, Aaron, who was born with birth defects created by chromosome damage. As we cried together, the Lord had me tell him this: "I just know that God has a good plan in all this. His plans are good. If you will run toward Him and not away from Him during this time, you'll see." Chris said, "Promise?" And, I could honestly answer with authority, "Yes, I've seen it."

I didn't realize until later that 6-1/2 years before, as I met people that told me the same thing, I had also asked, "Promise?" It seemed too good to be true, that great good could come from such horror, but I can tell you it is true. My dreams of a fulfilling, pleasing life have come true with God through relationship with Jesus Christ.

What I love about the Lord is that He can, and will, take the greatest pain of your life and turn it to good – good for you, good for others, and good for Him. He will break through to the hurt in your heart and bind it up, healing the pain so that you are not destroyed by it. The Word of God tells us, in Romans 8:28, 'And we know that all things work together for good to them that love God, to them who are called according to His purpose.' All things in themselves are not good, but God will work all things to the good. I love and appreciate Him for doing this with me.

I am amazed that He was able to break through to my hard heart, my screaming emotions, and my shattered life. I see

His power in it all. His hand was on me long before I knew Him.

And His hand was on Bob, too. One month before Bob's death, Tawny suggested that we attend a Harvest Crusade with her and her husband. I was not sure what a crusade was, and Bob was certainly not thrilled with the idea. He didn't want to be on a church bus with "those religious hypocrites". Having exhausted a collection of medical doctors and other experts and still desperate for something to work, I made him go anyway.

At the end of Pastor Greg Laurie's speech, he extended an invitation to pray the sinner's prayer. My heart had hardened during the end of the speech, so I was not reciting anything. So, I glanced over at my husband. His head was down, his eyes closed, and he was intently saying the prayer, repeating after the pastor word for word.

Assuming that we had both come to the Lord, Tawny asked me if we wanted to go down onto the field. She offered to go with us. I knew that my heart wasn't there, so I asked Bob, "Honey, do you wanna go down on the field?" He looked at me with the most different look I had ever seen in his eyes and stated matter-of-factly, "I don't have to go down on a field to know what's in my heart." I looked at him and saw something new that moment, but I didn't understand. He didn't understand either. In his depression, he died not knowing whether he was going to heaven or hell.

After I invited Jesus into my heart, I knew what his prayer meant. Although there is no marriage in heaven, I will one day be worshipping Jesus with my favorite people, and Bob will be one of them.

I do not know how Bob would have otherwise been saved. He wasn't receptive to people who came to our door or to studying about God. I practically had to force him onto the church bus, which was a miracle in itself because I didn't have much energy in those days. God saw to it that Bob heard the message of His love and responded to it. Praise be to God for His faithfulness.

It is the greatest gift of my tragedy to know that God was in the midst of it all along. He cared to see me whole, healed, and well. He cared for Bob, even though Bob didn't know it. This is true for you, too. If you will turn to Jesus and ask Him to be your Savior and Lord of your life, He will PROMISE to never let you go. The process of true healing will begin and He will see it through to completion. Many others and I have experienced His glorious touch on our hearts. May He be with you this day to guide you and love you.

As for Chris, his wife, Stephanie, gave birth to a healthy baby boy due on, of all days, Thanksgiving. Thanks be to God for His indescribable gifts.

The Lord has done great things for us, and we are filled with joy. (Psalm 126:3)

CHAPTER THIRTY-ONE:
LOVER OF MY SOUL

"I held him and would not let him go…"

"All night long on my bed I looked for the one my heart loves;
I looked for him but did not find him,
I will get up now and go about the city, through its streets and
squares;
I will search for the one my heart loves,
So I looked for him but did not find him."

(Song of Songs 3:1, 2)

As I moved through the first two years after Bob's suicide, this is what I was doing.

***

"The watchmen found me as they made their rounds
in the city."

(3:3)

God placed people on my path, His watchmen, as I moved about my life. I came into contact with them in parks, restaurants, at my doorstep, running errands, wherever I happened to be. I was so desperate in my search for God that the conversation would invariably lead to Him. At the end of these many conversations, I asked people, "What do you think I should read (or do) next?" I was ultimately asking how to find the One love that would make my heart right again.

***

"Have you seen the one my heart loves?"

(3:3)

My heart was seeking to replace Bob with another love, and I sensed that this love would have to be far greater than anything I had experienced on this earth. This is why men could not handle the job. It was far too great a task to fulfill. I needed the One who would love my WHOLE soul. I needed the One who would love my soul despite the hurts that had scarred it. I needed the One who would be soft with my soul, tender and merciful. I needed the One who would restore my soul with gentleness.

***

"Scarcely had I passed them when I found the one my heart loves. I held him and would not let him go…"

(3:4)

I found this lover of my soul in Jesus alone. Because He first found me and drew me to Himself, He is worth all I have in me to hold onto Him and never let Him go.

***

"All beautiful you are, my darling, there is no flaw in you."

(4:7)

This is what my Lord tells me now. You see, I needed the One who would love me despite the many flaws I saw in myself. I needed the One who viewed them differently. Because of what Jesus did on the cross for me, I am beautiful in God's sight. When God looks at me, He sees the beauty that Jesus left in me when He bore my ugliness on the cross. It was an uneven trade, but there is only beauty now…because of what Jesus gave.

CPSIA information can be obtained at www.ICGtesting.com
Printed in the USA
BVOW070059241012

303760BV00001B/21/A